California

Honey

Compliments

California Honey Advisory Board
P.O. Box 32
Whittier, Ca. 90608

Recipe Page 51

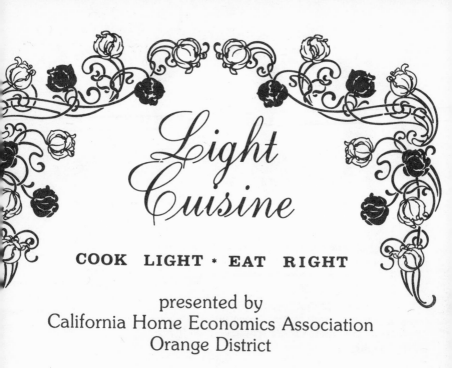

Light Cuisine

COOK LIGHT * EAT RIGHT

presented by
California Home Economics Association
Orange District

Editor: Carolyn S. Breeden
Editorial Assistant: Kathleen L. Brown
Nutrition Consultant: Avril Lovell, R. D.
Graphic Layout: Carolyn S. Breeden

©California Management Services MCMLXXIX
1115 E. Woodbury, Pasadena, California 91104
Library of Congress Catalog Card No. 79-54803
ISBN 0-89626-051-8

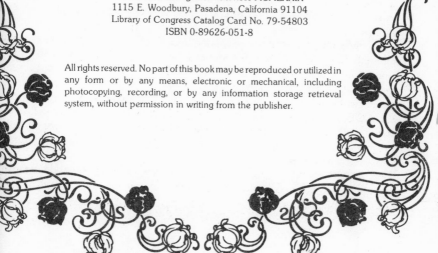

COOK LIGHT · EAT RIGHT

Light Cuisine can be the key to nutritious meals that start with a responsible, sensible approach to eating. It is filled with delicious, treasured recipes shared with you by members of the California Home Economics Association, Orange District. This gathering of favorites from professional home economists is not presented as a therapeutic cookbook. It is, rather, a collection of recipes rich in nutrients necessary to maintain a normal, healthy body. The ingredients are basic and the methods are simple in order that you may experience healthful, festive dining.

The professionals that have contributed these personal, kitchen-tested recipes are teachers, administrators, marketing directors, consumer service coordinators, consultants, dietitions, buyers, designers, and researchers. They work for food, clothing, and equipment companies; family parenting and child-care services; housing and interior design services; advisory boards; the cooperative extension service; governmental agencies; educational institutions; and some own their own businesses. They have been trained in the multi-disciplinary field of home economics with its focus on the family and its positive environment. The California Home Economics Association has a deep commitment to people and is involved in making communities better places to live. A continuing activity of the Orange District membership is to award scholarships to deserving home economics students, enabling them to continue their education. This is the second in a series of cookbooks conceived to raise funds for this purpose.

As editor, my philosophy in preparing this book for publication was to make minimal changes, clarifying in some instances and adding comments at the suggestion of our foods and nutrition consultant. There is no attempt on my part to suggest that all of the recipes are *extremely* light in calories. However, this criteria, within a sensible nutritional framework, was a high priority when recipes were chosen and edited. You should feel free to be creative and innovative just as the authors have undoubtedly been. Use these recipes to inspire your imagination and try some of the unique "recipe modification techniques" suggested within this book.

We hope these tasty, convenient, nutritious recipes guide you and help form wise eating habits for continued good health. Our wish for you is a pleasureable, healthful dining experience.

Carolyn Breeden
Editor

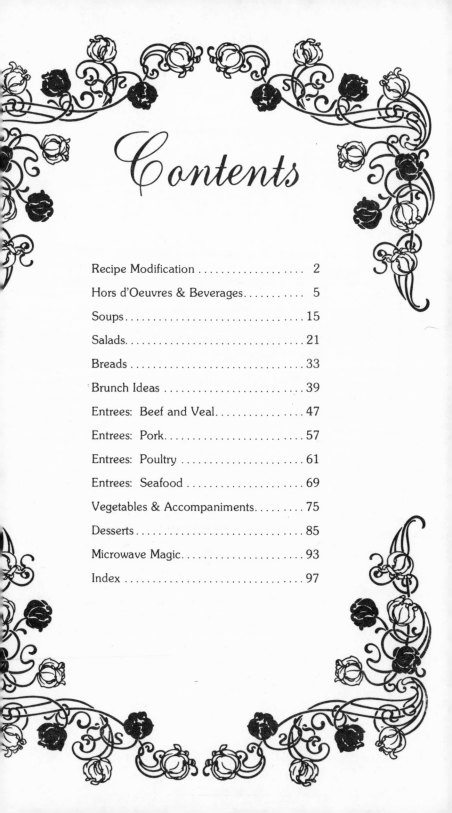

Contents

COLOR PHOTOGRAPH RECIPES

Beef and Shrimp Kabob

Morning Glory

Pineapple Cooler

Peach-Orange Spritzer

Honey French Dressing

Spinach Salad

Honey Bran Bud Muffins

Big John's Fresh Papaya Salad

Chinese Chicken

Virginia's Apple Tart

PHOTOGRAPHY CREDITS

Cover Photograph: Caryl Saunders Associates. Interior Photographs: California Honey Advisory Board, Sunkist Growers, Inc., Caryl Saunders Associates.

REORDER INFORMATION

Send name, address, and zip code to:

Carolyn Breeden

Family and Consumer Studies Department

Santa Ana College

17th at Bristol

Santa Ana, CA 92706

Recipe Modification

Recipe Modification

A sensible, light diet remains the solid foundation of weight control and consequent good health. Your choice of food should always be made on the basis of its high nutritional value in relation to its lowered calorie count. To approach your diet sensibly, it is essential that you take the time to learn some nutritional basics.

Although most foods contain several nutrients, there is not one food that contains them all. To get all the nutrients you need, you must eat a variety of foods. You may find it helpful to refer to a nutritional analysis chart or a *Basic Food Groups Guide* when estimating an adequate daily intake of each nutrient. Through careful planning, you can begin preparing calorie-trimmed meals that are satisfying *and* nutritious.

Weight control and good health can be more easily attained if you develop sound eating patterns, a responsible exercise program and an awareness of foods that provide ultimate nutrition. In addition, it is essential that a conscious effort be made to limit serving sizes. It has been wisely noted that if you practice portion control, you will not have to count calories.

Several techniques can be used to make calorie-trimming easier. Here are some gleaned from literature on weight control.

- *Eat slowly.* It becomes easier to tell when you have had enough to eat.
- *Restrict yourself to one eating area.* You will not have the opportunities to overeat.
- *Prepare low calorie snacks.* Keep a supply of filling, nutritious fresh fruits, vegetables and vegetable drinks on hand.
- *Don't shop when you are hungry.*
- *Preplan meals* and don't skip meals. Don't give yourself a chance to get overly hungry.
- *Plan pleasant activities* to occupy yourself when you have the urge to eat.
- *Stretch your meals.* Set aside a part of your normal meal. Eat several mini-meals during the day to help reduce eating additional foods.
- *Portion control.* Cut down on the size of portions. Use a smaller plate to make your meal look like more.

Although many elements other than calorie control are involved in the complex problem of weight control, it is still important that we learn ways of lowering calories. The following tips can help anyone successfully modify recipes.

To reduce calories and fats:

- Trim visible fat from meat and remove skin from poultry.
- Use non-stick sprays to coat pans.
- Brown meats by broiling rather than sauteing in fat.
- Chill soups and stews to lift off congealed fat.
- Use water packed canned fish.
- Use poultry, fish and veal in the place of red meats when appropriate.

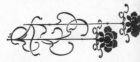

- Prepare vegetables with herbs and spices rather than adding fat or creamed sauces.

Substitutions:

Instead of	Use
• butter	low calorie margarine
• heavy cream	evaporated skim milk
• mayonnaise	low calorie mayonnaise
• whole milk	skim or non fat milk
• sour cream	plain low fat yogurt
• natural or process cheeses made with whole milk	skim milk cheeses or low fat cottage cheese
• whole eggs	egg whites only or egg substitute

Further Suggestions:

- In recipes for many baked products, the sugar can be reduced ⅓ to ¼ without harming the final product.
- Increasing the vanilla in recipes gives the impression of sweetness. Cinnamon also has the same effect.
- Add a pinch of salt for accent even with sugar to remove bland taste.
- Prepare gelatin desserts with a plain gelatin and unsweetened fruit juices instead of regular sweetened gelatin powders.
- If fruit is used, use fresh fruit preferably. However, if canned fruit is used, drain heavy syrup and rinse with water or use fruit packed in its own juice.
- Keep amount of thickening to a minimum.
- Substitute cornstarch for flour as you need only half as much to thicken.
- Make full use of herbs and low calorie seasoning agents such as vinegar, mustard, hot pepper sauce, etc., to sharpen taste. Fruit or tomato juice and fat-free bouillon may also be used.

In modification of most recipes, a certain amount of experimentation needs to take place. We urge you to be a bit daring and have some fun while you reduce calories in your favorite recipes. Cook light, eat right.

Hors d'Oeuvres and Beverages

Lumpia (from the Philippines)

1 pound ground pork (can substitute
   round steak, trimmed and ground)
2-3 tablespoons soy sauce
1 teaspoon MSG
1 teaspoon garlic powder
½ cup onions, minced

½ cup celery, minced
½ cup green beans, minced
½ cup carrots, minced
1 cup bean sprouts
1 pound wonton wrappers

Saute pork add soy sauce, MSG, and garlic powder. Cook 15-20 minutes. Add onions and celery and cook 5 minutes more. Add other ingredients (except wrappers) and cook 3-5 minutes more. Drain fat if necessary. Put about 1½ teaspoons of the mixture in each wrapper, and fold point at the bottom over filling and fold over each side and roll up. Wet all edges of wrapper with water to seal. At this point you can freeze them for future use or you can fry immediately. Fry in 1-inch of hot fat until lightly browned. Dip in soy sauce, Sweet Garlic Sauce or Sweet & Sour Sauce.

Sweet Garlic Sauce

1 cup brown sugar or brown sugar
   substitute
1½ cups water
1 clove garlic, minced
1 teaspoon MSG

1 teaspoon salt
½ teaspoon coarse ground pepper
2 teaspoons fresh ginger, chopped fine
3 tablespoons cornstarch
⅓ cup water

Simmer first 7 ingredients 15-20 minutes. Thicken with the cornstarch mixed in the ⅓ cup water. Stir and cook until clear. This may be kept for 4-6 weeks in the refrigerator if it isn't all used up.

A good appetizer for a patio party, guests can fry their own! Calories tend to be higher. Enjoy only one or two.

Lois Mock

Bacon Wrapper Water Chestnuts

1 can water chestnuts
1 pound bacon
Round toothpicks

6 ounces soy sauce
½ cup brown sugar (brown sugar substitute may be used)

Mix brown sugar and soy sauce. Wrap water chestnuts in bacon and secure with toothpicks. Marinate in soy sauce mixture overnight. Place wrapped chestnuts on cake rack over cookie sheet and bake at 300-350° F. until crisp.

Serve with other appetizers for a special treat! The bacon in this recipe raises the calorie count, so watch the number you enjoy.

Zelda Gerstner

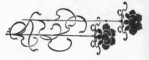

Tofu Guacamole Dip

½ cup tofu (soy bean curd), drained
2 ripe avocados
½ small onion, minced
1 clove garlic, minced
1 tablespoon lemon juice

1 teaspoon Worcestershire sauce
5 drops hot pepper sauce
1 teaspoon salt
½ teaspoon hot salsa

Whirl tofu in blender until smooth. Mash avocados. Add tofu and other ingredients to mashed avocados. Mix well. Press a piece of plastic wrap on the surface of the dip to prevent darkening. Chill. Serve as a dip for fresh vegetables. Also very good on lettuce as a salad. Makes 2 cups.

Reduced calories and increased nutrition. Calories per tablespoon: 24.

Betty R. Worden

"Guacamole"

1 large can cut asparagus, drained
1 package Ranch dressing (dry mix)
Juice of 1 lemon

1 tablespoon minced onion
1-2 drops hot pepper sauce or chopped
    chiles

Whip all ingredients in blender until smooth.

Extra low in calories! A simple meal and conversation starter.

Carolyn Trott

Salsa Jalapena

1 can (3.5 ounces) Ortega Jalapena
    "hot" chiles, whole
1 can (16 ounces) whole peeled tomatoes
    (drained)
1 garlic clove or ⅛ teaspoon garlic powder

1 medium onion
1 small bunch cilantro (can substitute
    parsley)
1 tablespoon vegetable oil
Salt to taste

Place chiles, tomatoes and garlic in electric blender. Push blend or liquify button for 2 seconds. Dice onion and chop small amount of cilantro or parsley. Add to mixture along with vegetable oil and salt. Blend for another 2 seconds or until salsa looks well mixed. You do not want it to be runny. Makes a lot, goes a long way.

Use with fresh vegetables or as a sauce on a Mexican omelette. Unlimited possibilities!

Jeannie Foley

Louisiana Shrimp Dip

6 ounces cream cheese with chives
2 tablespoons sour cream
2 tablespoons chili sauce
1 tablespoon lemon juice
1 teaspoon parsley, chopped

1 teaspoon horseradish
4 drops hot pepper sauce
½ teaspoon onion salt
1 can (4.25 ounces) of tiny cleaned shrimp

Rinse shrimp in water, drain and chop coarsely. Soften chive cheese in bowl, then beat with electric mixer. Gradually add sour cream, chili sauce and lemon juice. Mix until well blended. Add parsley, horseradish, hot pepper sauce and onion salt and combine thoroughly. Finally, add the chopped shrimp and stir. Store in refrigerator at least one hour before serving. Makes 2 cups.

This is a favorite that people ask me to bring to a potluck.

Florence Reid

Curried Almonds

2 cups whole blanched almonds
1 tablespoon butter

2 teaspoons seasoned salt
¾ teaspoon curry powder

Spread nuts in a shallow baking pan. Dot with butter. Bake in 350° F. oven about 20 minutes or until golden and toasty brown. When butter melts stir nuts or shake pan so they are evenly coated. Remove from oven. Blend the seasoned salt and curry powder in a mortar and pestle, then sprinkle over nuts. Stir thoroughly. Return to oven and continue baking several minutes for the seasoning to bake in. Remove from oven and spread on absorbent paper to cool. Makes 2 cups.

This recipe was developed for use at my niece's wedding reception. Delicious, but limit the number!

Mabel Southworth

Tabbouleh Dip

½ cup medium or fine bulgar (crushed wheat)
3 medium, fresh, ripe tomatoes, finely chopped
1 cup finely chopped parsley
1 cup finely chopped onions
¼ cup fresh lemon juice
2 teaspoons salt

¼ cup olive oil
2 tablespoons finely chopped fresh mint leaves or 1 tablespoon dried, crumbled mint
Romaine lettuce leaves
Cherry tomatoes or sliced black olives (optional)

Dippers

Pita bread cut into triangles
Celery pieces (cut crosswise)

Cauliflower (cut into small bite-size pieces)

Bulgar can be purchased at Middle Eastern grocery/deli stores or in the international sections of some supermarkets. Place the bulgar in a deep bowl. Add the tomatoes, parsley, onions, lemon juice, salt, olive oil and mint and combine thoroughly but gently. (An easy way to "chop" the parsley and fresh mint is to place it in a glass measuring cup and snip it with kitchen shears until the desired fineness is reached.) Cover bowl well and refrigerate mixture 1 hour or more. The bulgar will absorb much of the liquid. Before serving, line serving bowl with Romaine lettuce leaves. Use a slotted spoon to transfer the mixture to the serving bowl to eliminate unabsorbed liquid. Can garnish with cherry tomatoes or sliced black olives. Serve as a dip with pita bread triangles and cut up fresh vegetables such as celery, zucchini and cauliflower. Serves 4-6.

This is always a hit as a special party dip or outdoor picnics such as at the Hollywood Bowl. Also great wrapped in Romaine lettuce and served as a salad.

Barbara Gershman

Dilly Dip

1 tablespoon milk
⅔ cup low fat cottage cheese
⅔ cup imitation mayonnaise
1 tablespoon chopped green onion

1 tablespoon minced parsley
1 teaspoon dill weed
1 teaspoon beau monde seasoning

Pour milk in blender. Add cottage cheese; cover and blend until smooth. Add remaining ingredients to cottage cheese and mix. Chill at least 2 hours before serving. Serve with crisp fresh vegetables. Makes 1½ cups dip.

A great hit at parties, potlucks, or any get-together.

Carol Heinz-Dooley

Guacamole

2 ripe avocados
½-1 medium diced tomato (optional)
1 tablespoon finely diced red onion (or 1½ tablespoons finely diced green onion)

½-1 teaspoon hot green chili relish
1 tablespoon lemon juice
¼ teaspoon salt
¼ teaspoon garlic salt (or ¼ teaspoon garlic powder)

Mash avocados in blender, then add remaining ingredients and mix together. Serves 6.

Great with raw vegetables.

Ruth E. Jacobson

Eggplant Caviar

1 medium eggplant
2 ounces onion, finely chopped
3 cloves garlic, minced
1 medium tomato, peeled, chopped

1½ teaspoons vinegar
½ teaspoon salt
Dash hot sauce

9

Preheat oven to 350° F. Bake eggplant 30 minutes or until tender. Remove from oven and place in a bowl of cold water. Peel eggplant; combine 2 cups chopped eggplant with remaining ingredients in a medium bowl. Chill. Divide equally. Makes 2 servings.

This is so yummy and so low in calories that you can eat it by the cupful!

Roseanne M. Bye

Deviled Eggs Supreme

6 hard cooked eggs, halved lengthwise
1 can (2 ounces) deviled ham spread
2 tablespoons imitation mayonnaise
1 teaspoon prepared mustard
1 teaspoon vinegar
Dash pepper

Remove egg yolks; mash and combine with remaining ingredients. Refill egg whites using pastry tube, if desired. Makes 12 egg halves.

Makes an attractive and nutritious appetizer within calorie limitations!

Carol Heinz-Dooley

Pickled Onions

½ cup salt
3 cups cold water
2 pounds small white boiling onions, peeled
1 pint white vinegar
¼ cup dark brown sugar or brown sugar substitute
1 teaspoon whole allspice
1 teaspoon mustard seed
1 teaspoon black peppercorns
1 teaspoon mixed pickling spice

In large bowl, dissolve salt in water and add onions. Refrigerate 12 to 24 hours. Drain and rinse onions. Pack in wide mouth 1½ quart jar or crock. In a saucepan, bring the remainder of ingredients to a boil. Pour hot marinade over onions. Let cool, cover and refrigerate for a week before serving.

A great idea for an hors d'oeuvre, relish tray condiment, or a garnish for an entree.

Margie Chitwood

Pickled Eggs

12 eggs, hard cooked and peeled
2 cups cider vinegar
1 cup water
2 bay leaves
½ teaspoon ground allspice
2 teaspoons salt
20 yellow pickled peppers
4 ounces juice from pickled peppers
8 whole cloves
12 whole peppercorns
2 cloves garlic, minced

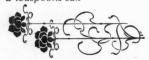 

Place eggs in large container. Add remaining ingredients and set in refrigerator for 2 to 3 days.

This recipe was developed by good friends after a lot of experimentation. If you like spicy, semi-hot food, you will really enjoy these. Low in calories.

Margie Chitwood

Pimiento Cheese Ball

2 ounces roasted and peeled green chiles (mild)
1 pound sharp natural Cheddar cheese
1 jar (2 ounces) pimiento, well drained
1 tablespoon water

1 package green onion dip mix, or ½ cup finely chopped green onion
½ cup imitation mayonnaise
¼ cup diet margarine

Rinse seeds from chiles. Grind chiles, Cheddar cheese and pimiento. Blend dip mix with water and add with mayonnaise and butter to the cheese mixture. Beat with electric mixer until thoroughly combined. To make one large cheese ball, butter small rounded bowl and pack well. Refrigerate until firm. Unmold when ready to serve and arrange assorted crackers or party rye on tray. Makes 3 cups.

Terrific for gift giving; pack cheese mixture in small crocks or pottery jars. Keep refrigerated. Tie up in holiday wrappings. Makes 6 small pots, ½ cup each.

Mabel Southworth

Beef Jerky

3 pounds lean round steak or Venison
1 tablespoon salt
1 teaspoon onion powder
1 teaspoon garlic powder

½ teaspoon pepper
⅓ cup Worcestershire sauce
¼ cup soy sauce

Freeze meat until it is almost solid. Make sure it is flat. Slice meat into very thin strips (½" wide X ¼" thick or thinner), each strip 4-6 inches long. Make sure all fat is trimmed off. Place meat in large glass or plastic bowl, casserole, or baking dish. Combine for marinade in separate bowl: salt, onion powder, garlic powder, pepper, Worcestershire sauce, soy sauce. Pour marinade over meat and let stand in refrigerator overnight. Make sure container is tightly covered. Gently turn or mix meat once or twice. Drain meat well and pat dry with paper towels to shorten the drying time. Place cooling racks on top of baking sheets with sides. (jelly roll pans). Takes approximately 3 baking sheets—or you can improvise with any type of shallow pan and rack arrangement. Dry meat in 175° F oven, 7-9 hours or until meat is dry, chewy, and fairly firm. Wipe out condensation on oven door every 1-2 hours. Turn meat once to get even drying. Check after 7 hours to determine doneness. When meat is done, cool thoroughly at room temperature. Put into clean jars with tight lids. Will keep well on shelf if meat has been thoroughly dried.

A family friend shared this recipe, although he always used his own Venison. It makes a great snack, appetizer, outdoor treat or gift.

Barbara Gershman

11

Vegetables with Yogurt Dip

Celery, zucchini, cauliflower
Jicama and carrot sticks
Broccoli flowers
Cucumber slices
Cherry tomatoes

Young onions and cauliflower
2 cups plain yogurt
½ cup chili sauce
¼ teaspoon garlic
¼ teaspoon finely crumbled dill weed

Wash, dry and trim vegetables; peel the carrots and jicama. Cut vegetables into pieces that are easy to handle for dipping and munching. Use only the broccoli flowers and split them into bite-size pieces. Run fork down side of cucumber before slicing. Whisk together yogurt, chili sauce, garlic and dill weed. Cover and chill until needed. Line a shallow basket with damp towels. Arrange vegetables in basket around a small dish for the yogurt dip. Cover with damp towel to keep vegetables fresh until needed. Fill dish with chilled dip just before serving.

Extra low in calories and high in nutrition. Takes the place of high-calorie snacks and appetizers.

Leone Ann Heuer

Hot Tomato Refresher

2 cans (24 ounce) vegetable juice cocktail
2 tablespoons lemon juice
2 tablespoons Worcestershire sauce

½ teaspoon ground allspice
Lemon slices

In a large pan combine vegetable juice cocktail, lemon juice, Worcestershire sauce, and allspice. Heat through. Just before serving, float lemon slices atop hot beverage, if desired. Makes 12 servings.

A refreshing treat for the waist! Only 35 calories per serving. Great substitute for the cocktail hour.

Carol Heinz-Dooley

Morning Glory

2 cups pineapple pink grapefruit juice
   drink, chilled
1 small, ripe banana

2 eggs
2 tablespoons sugar or 1 tablespoon honey
4 ice cubes

Combine ingredients in blender container. Cover and run on high until smooth and well blended. Pour into chilled glasses and serve immediately. Makes 2 (10 ounce) glasses or 6 juice glasses.

Attractive, delicious and nutritious breakfast drink.

Eileen Jo Jackson

Recipes for "Morning Glory," page 12; for "Strawberry Yogurt Drink," page 13; → for "Orange-Peach Spritzer," page 14.

Frozen Strawberry "Daiquiri"

1½ tablespoons lime juice
1 tablespoon rum extract
1 cup sliced strawberries, fresh

Sugar substitute to equal 1 tablespoon
 sugar
2 cups crushed ice

Place all ingredients in blender container. Cover and blend on high speed. As mixture freezes it will stop churning. Stop blender and stir with spatula from time to time. Pour into frosty glasses and garnish with whole berry. Serves 2.

Delicious non-alcoholic drink with the taste of the "real thing." Refreshing and light.

Carolyn Breeden

Strawberry-Yogurt Drink

1 half-gallon milk (lowfat or skim)
1 container (16 ounce) lowfat strawberry
 yogurt

1 container (8 ounce) lowfat strawberry yogurt
3 ripe bananas, peeled
Ice cubes

Mix ½ of each of the ingredients in electric blender with ice cubes. Pour into pitcher. Repeat. Serve over additional ice cubes as desired. It is best when it is icy cold, but not diluted. Serves 8-12.

During finals I surprised an early morning nutrition class with this quick beverage. It helped make up for missed breakfasts.

Barbara Gershman

Pineapple Cooler

½ cup canned crushed pineapple in its
 own juice, frozen
¾ cup nonfat milk

¼ teaspoon rum flavoring
pinch each nutmeg and cinnamon
Sugar substitute to equal 1-2 teaspoons

In blender jar combine all ingredients. Blend at high speed until just creamy and foamy. Pour into tall, slim glasses. Sprinkle foam with just a pinch of nutmeg. Serves 2.

Quite low in calories when sugar substitute is used. Rich tasting with only 110 calories total.

Virginia Witmer

13

← Recipes for "Spinach Salad" on page 28; for "Tossed Salad Italiano" on page 28.

Orange-Peach Spritzer

2 medium peaches, unpeeled
1 cup orange juice, freshly squeezed
½ cup lemon juice, freshly squeezed

Sugar substitute to equal ½ to 1 tablespoon
8 ice cubes

Slice and pit peaches. In blender container combine fruit juices, ice cubes, sweetener and peaches. Cover and blend until smooth. Pour into 2 glasses and garnish with additional fruit or mint sprigs. Serves 2.

Fast and cool on a warm day. Beautiful way to enjoy a summer sunset.

Carolyn Breeden

14

Soups

Cauliflower Soup

1 large cauliflower
6 cups water
6 cubes bouillon

2 tablespoons margarine
Salt and pepper to taste
Garnish of parsley flakes

Clean cauliflower, cut off leaves, and cut into small flowers and pieces. Put in kettle with water and bouillon cubes. Simmer until the cauliflower is soft. Blend in blender or put through sieve. Season. Garnish with a sprinkling of parsley flakes. Serves 4-6.

An almost calorieless "cream" soup.

Carolyn Trott

Watercress Soup

4 cups shredded Romaine lettuce
2 bunches watercress with stems
1 bunch scallions, cut into pieces
1 cup potatoes, peeled and diced

Salt and pepper to taste
4 cups chicken broth
½ cup heavy cream (substitute skimmed evaporated milk)

Combine Romaine with scallions, watercress and potatoes in a deep kettle. Add chicken broth and cook over high heat for 15 minutes, until vegetables are tender. Transfer soup to a blender and blend until smooth. Taste for salt and pepper. Add cream and serve hot or chilled. Serves 8.

I prefer to serve this soup cold on a hot evening and use it in place of a salad.

Alta Gruenwald

Chilled Hungarian Berry Soup

1 package (10-12 ounces) frozen blue-berries, strawberries or raspberries
¼ cup sweet Madeira (Malmsey) ruby Port or cream sherry
2 containers (8 ounces each) lowfat fruit yogurt

1 container (8 ounces) lowfat plain yogurt
1-4 tablespoons superfine sugar or as needed to taste

In a food processor fitted with the metal chopping blade, puree all but the sugar using two to three 30 second churnings of the motor (scrape work bowl down between churnings with a rubber spatula). Sweeten to taste with sugar, buzz 15 seconds longer, pour into stemmed goblets and garnish by floating an orange slice on each portion, adding a mint sprig and cluster of fresh berries. Serves 4-6.

Wonderful for an afternoon picker-upper. Nice to serve for dessert or at the beginning of a warm summer evening meal.

Alta Gruenwald

Low-Calorie Soup

1 small bunch celery
2 medium or large zucchini
2 tablespoons dehydrated onion flakes
1 tablespoon dehydrated parsley flakes

1 medium green pepper, diced
⅔ can tomato juice or vegetable juice
Bean sprouts (optional)
Beef bouillon

Cook celery in small amount of water, add zucchini, green pepper and more water, if necessary. Simmer about 15 minutes and add the onion flakes and parsley flakes and juice. Add beef bouillon to taste. The bean sprouts are added last and only simmered a few minutes. Makes 6-8 large servings.

I sometimes add 1 can string beans (French style) and find that it tastes better the longer it stands. . .a day or two. Great for snacks.

Zelda H. Gerstner

Greek Lemon Soup

5 cups chicken broth (3 cans)
½ cup raw rice
4 eggs

6 teaspoons lemon juice
6 slices lemon

Bring broth to a boil and add rice. Cook covered until rice is tender; remove from heat. Beat eggs until frothy, adding lemon juice by the tablespoon. Slowly add 1 cup of hot soup to mixture, beating constantly. Pour mixture into soup, still beating and serve immediately. Do not boil to reheat. Garnish with lemon slices. Serves 6.

A wonderful low-calorie beginning to a summertime meal. Also good when served in mugs in front of a cozy fireplace.

Joann Driggers

Oaks Onion Soup

5 medium onions, sliced thin
6 tablespoons beef bouillon or soup stock
6 cups boiling water

1 tablespoon soy sauce
2 tablespoons grated Parmesan cheese

Combine all ingredients except Parmesan cheese. Simmer 30 minutes. Sprinkle a little Parmesan on each serving. Makes 6 servings.

So simple to prepare, you'll make this many times—a satisfying way to begin a meal. 40 calories per serving.

Roseanne Bye

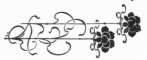

17

Cold Apricot Yogurt Soup

3 cups fresh apricots (about 1 pound can)
1½ cups fruity white wine
2-4 tablespoons low calorie preserves
1 pint plain lowfat yogurt

Milk (optional)
Toasted wheat germ
Apricot slices

Puree chopped apricots, wine and preserves in blender or food processor. Transfer to large bowl, whisk in yogurt; then with milk if necessary. Refrigerate and cover until cold, about 1 hour. Ladle soup into chilled bowls. Sprinkle with wheat germ; garnish with apricot slices.

I serve this in the summer instead of a salad. This is also a fantastic light dessert.

Alta Gruenwald

Gazpacho de Los Angeles

1 can (46 ounce) tomato juice
1 medium green pepper, minced
1 small onion, minced
1 cucumber, peeled and minced
2 small cans green chiles, minced
1 tablespoon Worcestershire sauce
1 teaspoon seasoned salt

1 teaspoon instant minced garlic
1 tablespoon olive oil
1 tablespoon chopped chives
2 drops hot pepper sauce
MSG (optional)
Salt, white pepper
Lemon wedges

Combine tomato juice, green pepper, onion, cucumber, chiles, Worcestershire, seasoned salt, garlic, oil, chives and hot pepper sauce. Season to taste with MSG, salt and white pepper. Chill thoroughly. Serve with lemon wedges. Makes 6 servings.

Note: For a smooth gazpacho served with vegetable garnishes, blend tomato mixture in blender until smooth. Serve with additional diced cucumber, green pepper and croutons on the side.

Hearty and low in calories!

Margie Chitwood

Gazpacho Soup

2 tablespoons garlic, minced
2 tablespoons celery, finely chopped
2 tablespoons lemon juice
4 tablespoons olive oil
½ teaspoon white wine vinegar
1 can (6 ounce) tomato juice cocktail
1 can (6 ounce) tomato juice
4 very ripe tomatoes, peeled and chopped

1 small cucumber, peeled, seeded and
   chopped
1 green pepper, chopped
2 small zucchini squash, finely chopped
1 medium white onion, chopped
Salt to taste
6 ice cubes

In a 2-quart container, mix all ingredients together. Stir very well. Chill. Makes 1½ quarts.

This cold soup idea is from Spain. Serve with a warm bread.

Sharyl Heavin

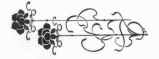

18

Pumpkin Soup

1 large onion (approximately 1 cup, sliced)
2 tablespoons margarine
2 cans (10¾ ounces each) chicken broth
1 can (16 ounce) pumpkin
1 teaspoon salt
¾ teaspoon ground cinnamon

¼ teaspoon ground nutmeg
⅛ teaspoon pepper
1 cup (½ pint) half and half or milk (use half and half for richer taste or milk to cut calories)

Saute onion in margarine in a large saucepan until onion is soft and clear, about 5 minutes. Add 1 can of the chicken broth (1⅔ cup). Bring to boil. Cover, lower heat and simmer 10 minutes. Put ½ cup of the onion/broth mixture in electric blender or food processor. Cover and blend until smooth. Add remaining onion/broth mixture and blend until smooth. Pour smooth mixture back into saucepan. Add remaining can of chicken broth, pumpkin, salt, cinnamon, nutmeg and pepper. Stir until smooth. Bring to a boil. Cover, lower heat, and simmer 10 minutes. Slowly stir in half and half or milk. Heat just until thoroughly hot. Makes 8 servings.

Note: Can be made ahead and refrigerated if half and half or milk is not added until close to serving time. The soup can then be reheated.

A student shared this recipe for our annual foods class Thanksgiving feast. It was a tremendous hit!

Barbara Gershman

Tomato Soup with Orange

2 pounds ripe tomatoes
1 tablespoon butter
1 medium onion, chopped
1 medium carrot, chopped
1 teaspoon dry basil

1 teaspoon sugar
2 chicken bouillon cubes
1 cup orange juice
Salt and pepper to taste
Thinly sliced whole orange (optional)

Cut out cores and chop tomatoes. (should have about 5 cups) Heat butter over medium heat in a 3-quart pan. Add onion and saute until limp. Add tomatoes, carrot, basil, sugar and bouillon cubes. Bring to boiling, then reduce heat, cover and simmer, stirring several times until carrot is tender; about 15 minutes. Remove from heat and whirl in a blender, about half the mixture at a time, until smooth. Return to pan, add orange juice, and reheat until hot. Season with salt and pepper. Serve with slices of orange on top. Serves 6.

The tomato and orange combination gives a unique and interesting flavor.

Bonnie Rader

19

Green Banana Soup

1 large onion, chopped
2 tablespoons butter or margarine
2½ teaspoons chili powder
½ teaspoon garlic salt
¼ teaspoon cumin
½ teaspoon oregano
1 can (1 pound, 12 ounce) whole tomatoes

1 can (15½ ounce) kidney beans
2 cups beef broth
2 cups diced cooked pork or beef or 1
   pound cooked round steak, trimmed
   and ground
2 green bananas
Grated Cheddar cheese

In a large kettle saute onion in butter until tender. Stir in chili powder, garlic salt, cumin and oregano. Cook 1 minute. Add undrained tomatoes, undrained kidney beans and beef broth. Bring to a boil. Cover and simmer 20 minutes. Cut bananas through the peel into chunks. Remove peel from each section, then slice bananas and add to soup. Cover and simmer 30 minutes longer. At serving time, sprinkle the soup sparingly with grated cheese. Serves 6-8.

This soup is good in cold weather.

Donna Gough

Salads

Chinese Chicken Salad

1 chicken breast, cooked and shredded
1 avocado, sliced

1 head lettuce, shredded
4 ounces rice sticks, fried

Dressing:

6 tablespoons rice vinegar
4 tablespoons soy sauce

4 tablespoons sugar
1 teaspoon dry mustard

Place shredded lettuce in individual salad bowls. Top with chicken and avocado. Mix all ingredients for dressing together and shake well. Serve fried rice sticks in large bowl at the table. Allow diners to help themselves to the rice sticks and dressing. Serves 4.

This was served to me after a first course of cold tomato soup garnished with melon balls, rolled in sweet basil. It was a wonderful combination which I now use to delight my guests.

Margie Chitwood

Big John's Fresh Papaya Salad

Fresh Papaya
1 pound fresh crab meat
1 small fresh bell pepper
2 stalks celery

2 green onions (½ of tops included)
1 orange
1 kiwi fruit
Salt

Chop green pepper and celery to ¼-inch dice. Thinly slice green onions. Peel and section orange. Peel and slice kiwi. Halve the papaya, remove seeds. Leaving about ¼-inch of flesh in the shell, remove the rest of the flesh. Cut in ½-inch dice. Combine the green pepper, celery, green onion and crab meat with the papaya. Season to taste. Fill the papaya shells and garnish with the orange sections and sliced kiwi. Top with honey french dressing. Serves 1-2.

Serve with Honey Bran Muffins and whipped honey butter for a delicious light meal.

Garry Johnston

Marinated Carrot Salad

2 pounds carrots, sliced and cooked
1 small green pepper, chopped
1 medium onion, sliced
1 can (10¾ ounce) tomato soup
⅓ cup oil
⅔ cup white vinegar
¾ cup sugar (or equivalent amount of
    sugar substitute)

1 tablespoon prepared mustard
1 tablespoon Worcestershire sauce
1 teaspoon garlic salt
Dash pepper
1½ teaspoons parsley, chopped

Combine carrots, green pepper and onion. Mix remaining ingredients, except for parsley, together and heat to boiling point. Pour over carrot mixture and allow to marinate several hours. Garnish with chopped parsley at serving time. Serves 6-8.

This salad keeps well refrigerated for several days. Remember not to overcook the carrots so they remain crunchy.

Margie Chitwood

Winter Tomato Salad

1 small cauliflower, separated
1 can (16 ounce) tomato wedges, drained
½ cup chopped onion
1 tablespoon vinegar

1 teaspoon seasoned salt
¼ teaspoon pepper
6 lettuce cups

Toss all ingredients except lettuce cups in bowl. Cover and refrigerate at least 30 minutes. With slotted spoon, remove vegetables to lettuce cups. Makes 6 servings, ¾ cup each.

Light and nutritious with only 35 calories per serving.

Carol Heinz-Dooley

Tofu Tossed Salad

1 bunch red leaf lettuce, torn into bite-size pieces
1 container alfalfa sprouts
1 small jicama, peeled and sliced into julienne strips
½ dill pickle, chopped
1 tablespoon or more, cilantro, torn or snipped into small pieces
1 jar (6 ounces) marinated artichoke hearts, drained

2 zucchini, sliced
2 or more green onions, minced
¼ pound mushrooms, sliced
2 ripe tomatoes, sliced
1 container fresh Tofu (soybean curd), cut into small squares
Favorite salad dressing

Combine all salad ingredients. Be sure to drain tofu well before adding to salad. Add your favorite salad dressing and toss well just before serving. An Italian, herb, or other oil and vinegar type dressing goes well with this salad. Optional ingredients which may be added are: cooked shrimp, crab, canned salmon, or leftover, cooked chicken. Serves 6.

This is an unusual and tasty way to serve tofu. The bland flavored tofu picks up the stronger flavors of the other salad ingredients. Serve with low-calorie dressing or none.

Barbara Gershman

23

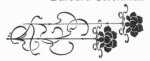

Salmon-Citrus Salad

1 carton (8 ounces) unflavored lowfat
 yogurt (1 cup)
1 tablespoon grated grapefruit peel
½ teaspoon salt
3 cups spinach, torn in bite-size pieces
1 cup celery, cut in thin diagonal slices
1 can (16 ounces) salmon, cleaned, drained
 and broken into pieces

1 grapefruit, pared and sectioned
1 teaspoon seasoned salt
1 tablespoon tarragon vinegar
Romaine lettuce leaves
Paprika

Mix yogurt, grapefruit peel and salt in small bowl; cover and refrigerate until serving time. Toss remaining ingredients except Romaine leaves and paprika. Turn salad into bowl lined with Romaine leaves; sprinkle with paprika. Serve with yogurt dressing. Makes 6, 1 cup servings.

A marvelous main-dish salad, even more tempting with only 145 calories per serving.

Janis L. Parks

Tuna Pineapple Boats

1 pineapple
2 cans (7 ounces each) white tuna in
 water, drained and broken into chunks
1 cup strawberries (reserve 4 whole berries
 for garnish), sliced
2 cups cantaloupe or honeydew melon
 balls

¼ teaspoon ginger
2 tablespoons lime juice
2 tablespoons dry roasted almonds,
 coarsely chopped
Dash ginger
Pineapple lowfat yogurt

Select a pineapple with fresh green leaves. Cut pineapple lengthwise into quarters through green top. Cut along curved edges of quarters with grapefruit knife to remove fruit. Cut fruit into chunks; remove core. Drain fruit and invert shells to drain. Place pineapple chunks, tuna, sliced strawberries and melon balls in large bowl. Sprinkle with ¼ teaspoon ginger and the lime juice and toss. Cover and refrigerate 1 hour. Spoon pineapple mixture into shells; sprinkle with almonds and a dash of ginger. Spoon 1 tablespoon yogurt onto each serving and garnish with reserved whole strawberries. Serves 4.

Can use cooked chicken or turkey in place of tuna. Makes a light, colorful meal.

Carol Heinz-Dooley

Holiday Salad Bowl

¼ cup almonds, slivered
3 medium oranges, peeled and sliced
1 small mild white onion, thinly sliced
1 cup red grapes, halved and seeded

1 medium cucumber, thinly sliced
¼ cup golden raisins
1 pomegranate
1 bunch spinach

Spread almonds in a shallow pan and place in a 350° F. oven for 8 minutes or until golden. Combine the oranges, onion, grapes, cucumber and raisins. Chill until serving time. Remove seeds from pomegranate. Prepare dressing by mixing all ingredients together. Tear spinach into bite size pieces. To serve: Combine orange mixture, spinach, and almonds in large bowl. Toss with dressing. Garnish with pomegranate seeds. Serves 6-8.

Lime Dressing:

¼ cup salad oil
¼ cup lime juice
1 clove garlic, minced or pressed
½ teaspoon curry powder

½ teaspoon paprika
¼ teaspoon cayenne
Salt to taste

This salad was served to me by a home economist friend, Anne Fortini. Since then, it has been a favorite for many of my guests.

Margie Chitwood

Tofu Fruit Salad

1 cup Tofu (soybean curd), diced
1 banana, sliced
1 can (11 ounce) mandarin oranges, drained
¾ cup green grapes

1 jar (8 ounce) maraschino cherries, drained
¾ cup pineapple chunks, drained
⅛ cup defrosted orange juice or lemonade concentrate

Prepare all fruits for salad. Very carefully toss all fruits and tofu with the concentrate. Do not mash the tofu. Chill well. Serves 6.

High nutrition and low calorie. Any colorful combination of fruits can be used.

Betty Worden

Chinese String Bean Salad

1 pound fresh string beans
1 tablespoon dried shrimp (optional), washed and soaked in 1 tablespoon water

1 clove garlic, chopped fine

Remove the ends and string from beans. Cut in half or thirds. In a saucepan bring 1 cup water to a boil and drop beans into it. Cook for 8-10 minutes until cooked but not soft. Drain beans and transfer to a serving bowl. Add shrimp and garlic. Mix dressing ingredients well and toss with beans. Cover and refrigerate for 1 hour or until well chilled before serving. Serves 4-6.

Dressing:

1 tablespoon sugar
1 tablespoon vinegar
1 teaspoon soy sauce

1 teaspoon salt
1 tablespoon sesame oil

This is a crisp salad and low caloried! *Serve in a hollow tomato for added color.*

Eleanor Widolf

Orange Wedges

6 medium oranges
1 package (3 ounce) orange flavored diet
   gelatin

½ cup boiling water
1 can (8½ ounce) crushed pineapple
Lettuce

Cut oranges in half lengthwise, from stem to bud end. Scoop out pulp. Squeeze juice from pulp; put aside 1 cup juice. Dissolve gelatin in boiling water. Add crushed pineapple and juice. Pour into orange shells. Chill until firm. To serve, cut oranges into wedges and arrange on a bed of lettuce. Makes 48 wedges.

Different, fun and cool salad idea.

Florence Reid

"Sour Cream" Dressing

1 cup low fat cottage cheese

⅓ cup buttermilk

Whip in blender until smooth.

This is an acceptable substitution in any dip, garnish, topping, or recipe where sour cream is called for, in order to halve the calories.

Carolyn Trott

Light Weight Sour Cream

¼ cup nonfat milk
1 cup lowfat cottage cheese
Noncaloric sweetener

1 tablespoon lemon juice
Salt

Combine milk, cottage cheese, lemon juice and salt to taste in blender container. Blend until smooth. Add sweetener to taste. Makes about 1 cup.

12 calories per tablespoon. A great substitute for the real thing!

Carol Heinz-Dooley

26

Honey French Dressing

1 can (10½ ounce) tomato soup
¼ cup honey
½ cup vinegar or lemon juice
¼ cup salad oil

1 teaspoon salt
1 teaspoon dry mustard
½ teaspoon black pepper

Mix all ingredients in blender or mixer bowl. Blend or beat until smooth. Good keeper in refrigerator. Makes 1 pint.

Easy as 1, 2, 3. Zips up salad greens! Delicious, but use sparingly.

Mona Schafer Reed

Lo-Cal Salad Dressing

1 cup tomato juice
2 tablespoons lemon juice
1 thin onion slice
1 teaspoon prepared mustard
¼ teaspoon salt

½ teaspoon celery seed
Dash hot pepper sauce
2 teaspoons Worcestershire sauce
4-6 drops noncaloric sweetener

Blend in a blender container.

Only 3 calories per tablespoon. Makes a good basting sauce for meats also.

Carol Heinz-Dooley

Wonton Salad

4 chicken breasts, boned, skinned and
    shredded
1 bunch celery, chopped
1 bunch scallions, diced
1 head lettuce, shredded

1 package wonton skins
Brown sugar
Red vinegar
Oriental sesame seed oil

Combine chicken, celery, scallions and lettuce. Fry wonton skins in oil and drain on paper towel. For the dressing, combine equal parts of brown sugar, red vinegar and sesame seed oil. Add the dressing to the salad and toss well. Add the fried wonton skins after tossing and serve. Serves 8.

Excellent for a warm afternoon ladies luncheon main dish.

Alta Gruenwald

Marinated Avocado-Mushroom Salad

2 medium avocados, seeded, peeled and
    sliced
1 cup sliced fresh mushrooms
2 thin slices onion, separated in rings
¼ cup salad oil
¼ cup dry white wine

2 tablespoons vinegar
½ teaspoon sugar
¼ teaspoon salt
¼ teaspoon dried basil, crumbled
Bibb lettuce leaves

27

In bowl, combine avocado, mushrooms and onion rings. In screw top jar combine oil, wine, vinegar, sugar, salt and basil; shake well. Pour over vegetables. Cover and chill for 2-3 hours, stirring occasionally. Drain avocado mixture. Serve on lettuce leaves. Serves 4.

This salad adds an elegant, gourmet touch to your meal.

Eileen Jo Jackson

Spinach Salad

4 bunches spinach
4 slices bacon, cooked crisp and crumbled
1 small Bermuda onion, sliced
¼ cup celery, diced
4 hard boiled eggs, sliced

1 cup plain lowfat yogurt
1 package garlic cheese salad dressing
 mix
3 tablespoons lemon juice
Salt and pepper to taste

Wash, dry and tear the spinach into bite-size pieces. Combine with the crumbled bacon, onion, celery and eggs. Toss and refrigerate. Mix rest of ingredients for the dressing in a separate bowl. Use half of the dressing for the salad. Refrigerate remaining dressing for future use. Serves 8.

Refreshing, low calorie accompaniment to any light meal.

Carolyn Breeder

Kumquat Avocado Salad

1½ package (3 ounce) lemon flavored
 diet gelatin
¾ cup very hot water
1¼ cup diet gingerale, chilled

¼ teaspoon salt
½ cup kumquats, seeded and thinly sliced
2 ripe avocados
¼ cup kumquat syrup

Dissolve gelatin in very hot water. Add chilled gingerale and salt. When this mixture has thickened (not completely set), add sliced avocados, kumquats and kumquat syrup. Chill several hours until well set. Serves 6-8.

Do not add any extra liquid. Good salad for festive occasions.

Sylvia Kern

Tossed Salad Italiano

1 package (9 ounce) frozen Italian green
 beans, cooked, drained and cooled
1 pound small zucchini (about 4) cut into
 ¼" slices
1 small onion, thinly sliced

1 cup cherry tomatoes, cut in half
¼ teaspoon garlic salt
½ cup low-calorie Italian dressing
2 tablespoons Mozzarella cheese

Combine vegetables in bowl and sprinkle with garlic salt. Pour dressing over vegetables and toss. Sprinkle with cheese on top. Serves 6.

Use herb flavored vinegar, no fat or zero calorie salad dressing. 40 calories per serving

Carol Heinz-Dooley

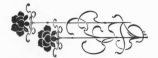

Recipe for "Honey Bran Bud Muffins" on page 35 —

Hot Spiced Fruit Salad

1 can (1 pound each) peach halves; pear halves; apricot halves; pineapple chunks; pitted, light sweet cherries
2 tart apples, peeled, cored and cubed
Juice of 1 lemon
½ teaspoon ground nutmeg
½ teaspoon ground cinnamon
¼ teaspoon ground cloves
⅓ cup brown sugar or brown sugar substitute
¼ cup butter or margarine
2 cups fresh seedless grapes
3 bananas, peeled and sliced

Preheat electric oven to 325°. Drain the syrup from the canned fruit saving ½ cup. Place the canned fruits and apples into a 2½ quart casserole. Add lemon juice, seasoning, and sugar to the reserve fruit syrup; pour over the fruit. Dot fruit with butter. Cover and bake for 20 minutes. Fold in grapes and bananas. Cover and continue baking for an additional 5 minutes. Serve hot. Serves 12.

This is nice served as a side dish with a brunch meal.

Carol Heinz-Dooley

Cabbage-Apple Slaw

2 red delicious apples
½ head cabbage
1½-2 cups lowfat cottage cheese
3-4 tablespoons roasted, salted sunflower seeds

Core apples and cut into bite-size chunks. Chop cabbage into bite-size pieces, not too small. Combine apples and cabbage in large bowl. Mix in cottage cheese and sunflower seeds. (Prepare as close to serving time as possible so that apples will not darken). Serves 4.

This recipe, from my sister, is a nice change from a traditional slaw. It needs no other dressing.

Barbara Gershman

Hot Asparagus Salad

2 pounds asparagus, trimmed
1 teaspoon salt
Chive dressing (see below)
Chopped chives
Lemon slices

Cook asparagus in 1 inch boiling, salted water 10-15 minutes or until crisp-tender. Drain and serve hot with Chive Dressing. Garnish with chopped chives and lemon slices. Serves 6.

Chive Dressing:

⅓ cup sour cream or plain lowfat yogurt
¼ cup mayonnaise, low calorie
1½ tablespoons chives, chopped
1 tablespoon lemon juice
¼ teaspoon salt
¼ teaspoon dry mustard

← Recipe for "Fresh Papaya Salad" on page 22.

Combine ingredients in saucepan. Heat just until warm. Serve over asparagus spears.

A yummy way to serve asparagus during its short season. Frozen spears may be used when fresh ones are not available.

Eileen Jo Jackson

Green Pea Salad

1 package frozen peas
½ green pepper, diced
¼ pound cheese cubes (substitute lowfat
   pasteurized cheese)

¼ cup pickle relish
¼ cup parsley, minced
1 red onion, sliced

Dressing:

1 cup sour cream (or plain lowfat yogurt)
3 tablespoons vinegar
2 tablespoons sugar

1½ teaspoons salt
½ teaspoon dry mustard

Place peas in colander and rinse with hot water. Combine with rest of ingredients, and refrigerate. Make dressing and toss just before serving. Reserve a couple of onion rings for garnish. Serves 6-8.

A real quicky and always a success!

Karen Lindstrom-Titus

Hot Turkey or Chicken Salad

2 cups chicken or turkey, cooked and
   cubed
2 cups celery, sliced or chopped
¼ cup jicama, chopped

2 teaspoons onion, grated
1 teaspoon soy sauce
¼ cup low calorie mayonnaise
½ cup Cheddar cheese, grated

Combine all ingredients except cheese, and mix together. Spoon lightly into a baking dish. Sprinkle with cheese and bake at 450° F. for 10-15 minutes or until heated through. Serves 6.

Our guests enjoy this for lunch, and it is a delicious way to use leftover turkey. 149 calories per serving.

Roseanne Bye

Creamy Cole Slaw

1 medium cabbage, shredded
3 medium carrots, grated

2 tablespoons green pepper, finely chopped
2 tablespoons green onion, thinly sliced

Dressing:

½ cup imitation mayonnaise
½ teaspoon salt
Dash of seasoned pepper
Dash of paprika

2 tablespoons sugar
1 tablespoon vinegar
1 tablespoon milk

Prepare vegetables. Place in large bowl. Place all dressing ingredients in 2-cup glass measure. Blend until smooth. Pour over vegetables. Toss until vegetables are well-coated. Serves 6.

This slaw is great with soup and French bread. Keep leftovers in a tightly covered container. It will keep well for several days.

Eunice Bryant

Jellied Gazpacho Salad

2 envelopes unflavored gelatin
3½ cups tomato juice
2 tablespoons lemon juice
2 tablespoons vinegar

1 package Italian salad dressing mix
1 cup cucumber, finely chopped
1 cup tomato, finely chopped
½ cup green pepper, minced

Sprinkle gelatin over 2 cups of the tomato juice in saucepan. Place over low heat and stir constantly until dissolved, about 3 minutes. Remove from heat and add remaining 1½ cups tomato juice, lemon juice and vinegar. Stir gently. Add Italian salad dressing mix and blend. Cool and refrigerate until slightly thickened. Add chopped vegetables (well drained) to tomato mixture and stir gently. Turn into a 6-cup mold or 12 individual molds. Chill until set, preferably overnight. Unmold and garnish with parsley, watercress or lettuce as desired. Serves 12.

Note: For salad dressing use ½ cup imitation mayonnaise and ½ cup sour cream. (or plain lowfat yogurt. Blend and thin with a little lemon juice.)

This recipe was created to have the flavors of the popular soup, but in a form easier to manage for a dinner party or a buffet supper.

Mabel Southworth

Breads

Calorie Saving Waffles

Dash salt
2 egg whites
¼ teaspoon salt

¾ cup skim milk
¾ cup cake flour
2 teaspoons baking powder

Sprinkle dash of salt on egg whites and beat until stiff, but not dry. Place milk, flour and salt in electric blender. Blend a few seconds until smooth. Add baking powder and blend for two seconds. Fold egg whites lightly into batter. Cook until crisp in preheated waffle iron without stirring the batter. These waffles take longer to cook than regular waffles. Makes 8-10 waffles or 15 pancakes.

These pancakes or waffles have 26 calories each, whereas traditional waffles have 215 calories per section.

Carol Heinz-Dooley

Wheat Germ Snack Sticks

¾ cup flour
½ cup wheat germ
1 teaspoon baking powder
½ teaspoon salt
2 tablespoons sesame seeds

¼ cup diet margarine
4-5 tablespoons water
Egg wash (1 egg and 1 tablespoon water
    mixed together)
¼ cup Parmesan cheese, grated

Mix flour with wheat germ, baking powder, salt and sesame seeds. Cut in margarine with pastry blender. Sprinkle with water, tossing with fork until dough forms a ball. Divide dough in half. Roll each half on lightly floured surface to a 12-inch square. Brush with Egg wash. Sprinkle with cheese. Cut into 4" x 1½" strips. Place on greased baking sheet. Bake at 375° F. 8-10 minutes, or until light golden and crisp. Remove from baking sheet and cool on rack. Store in container with loose fitting cover. Makes 4 dozen.

Delicious served with soup or salad or by itself as a nutritious snack. Each stick contains about 26 calories.

Eileen Jo Jackson

Special Whole Wheat Bread

4-4½ cups all-purpose flour
2 cups whole wheat flour
2 packages instant blend dry yeast
1 tablespoon salt
1½ cups lowfat milk

½ cup water
½ cup small curd cottage cheese
¼ cup honey
¼ cup butter or diet margarine

Preheat oven to 375° F. In large mixer bowl, combine 1 cup all-purpose flour, whole wheat flour, yeast and salt; mix well. In saucepan, heat milk, water, cottage cheese, honey and butter until warm (120-130°); butter does not need to melt. Add to flour mixture. Blend at low speed until moistened. Beat 3 minutes at medium speed. By hand, gradually stir in remaining all-purpose flour to make

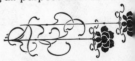

firm dough. Knead on floured surface until smooth and elastic, about 5 minutes. Place in greased bowl, turning to grease top. Cover; let rise in warm place until light and doubled, about 1 hour. Punch down dough. Divide into 2 parts. On lightly floured surface, roll or pat each half to a 14" x 7" rectangle. Starting with shorter side, roll up tightly, pressing dough into roll with each turn. Pinch edges and ends to seal. Place in greased 9"x5" loaf pans. Cover; let rise in warm place until light and doubled, about 1 hour. Bake at 375° F. for 35-40 minutes until golden brown and loaves sound hollow when tapped. Remove from pans and cool. Makes 2 loaves.

Special texture and delicious flavor. This would be a welcome gift for a treasured friend.
Milly Powell

Commuter Muffins

½ cup diet margarine
⅔ cup sugar (or less) or ½ cup honey
3 eggs
5 medium-size, ripe bananas
2 apples, cored and sliced (unpeeled) or ½ cup unsweetened applesauce
1 cup whole wheat flour
½ cup powdered nonfat dry milk (or more)

1 cup untoasted wheat germ
1-2 cups bran
1 cup 7 grain hot cereal
1 teaspoon baking soda
⅛ teaspoon salt
¾ cup dried currants or raisins (or 6 ounces mixed, chopped fruit)

Can make in food processor or electric mixer (large size food processor preferred, with metal chopping blade). Mix margarine, sugar or honey, and eggs until smooth. Add bananas and apples and mix until apples are coarsely chopped. (Mash bananas and chop apples first if using an electric mixer.) Add flour, nonfat dry milk, wheat germ and bran and mix well. Stir in or mix in dried fruit. Spoon into paper muffin cups in muffin tins. Bake in preheated 350° F. oven for 25-30 minutes or until toothpick comes out clean when muffins are tested. When cool, package in small freezer bags. Draw out excess air from bags with a straw before closing. Freeze until needed. (Can substitute other fruits in this recipe as desired.) Makes 24 large or 36 small muffins. (110 calories each.)

I developed this recipe as a commuter breakfast for my husband who has an hour commute each morning. He takes juice in a small travel thermos and chunks of cheese to round out the meal. He still likes the muffins after eating hundreds of them!
Barbara Gershman

Honey Bran Bud Muffins

2 cups bran buds
1 cup boiling water
2½ cups sifted flour
2½ teaspoons soda
½ teaspoon salt
2 eggs

¾ cup honey
½ cup oil
1¾ cups buttermilk
1 cup all bran
½ cup raisins (optional)
½ cup nuts (optional)

35

Pour boiling water over bran buds, let stand. Sift flour, add soda and salt. Beat eggs; add honey and oil. Add buttermilk, all bran, bran buds, and flour mixture in order given. Bake at 350° F. for 20-25 minutes. 2-2½ dozen.

Mixture will keep up to 5 weeks stored in refrigerator. Bake as needed. Experiment with additional ingredients for variety. Without nuts and raisins, these muffins contain only 117 calories each.

Helen F. Utley

Easy Bread

4 teaspoons dry yeast
⅔ cup lukewarm water
2 teaspoons honey
5 cups stone ground whole wheat flour
⅔ cup lukewarm water

3 tablespoons molasses
1⅓ cup lukewarm water
⅓ cup unprocessed bran
1 tablespoon sesame, chia or poppy seeds

Combine yeast, ⅔ cup water and honey in a bowl. Measure flour into large bowl and place in 250° F. oven for 20 minutes. Combine ⅔ cup water and molasses and add to yeast mixture. Add liquid mixture to flour and mix well. Add 1⅓ cup water, unprocessed bran and seeds and continue to mix well. Spray two 4" x 8" bread pans with nonstick spray. Pour batter into pans and leave to rise in a warm location for 45 minutes to an hour. Bake in a 425° F. oven for 50 minutes or until done. Remove bread from pan immediately and cool on a rack. Makes 2 loaves, 32 slices per loaf.

A tasty salt free bread with only 35 calories per slice. Recipe adapted from Recipes For Fitness *by Eleanor Brown—The Palms at Palm Springs.*

Bonnie Rader

Zucchini Bread

3 eggs
2 cups sugar
1 cup oil
3 cups raw zucchini, peeled and grated
1 tablespoon vanilla
3 cups flour

1 teaspoon salt
1 teaspoon baking soda
¼ teaspoon baking powder
1 tablespoon cinnamon
1 cup chopped walnuts

Beat the eggs until light and foamy. Add the sugar, oil, zucchini and vanilla. Mix lightly. Combine the dry ingredients and add to the zucchini/egg mixture. Stir until well blended. Fold in walnuts. Pour into two prepared loaf pans. Bake in preheated 350° F. oven for 55-60 minutes. Cool on a rack. Makes 2 loaves.

It is easy to make and tastes great! Slice thin for additional calorie savings.

Bonnie Landin

Super Bran Muffins

1 heaping cup shortening
2 cups sugar (or can substitute 1⅓ cups
   honey & molasses combined)
5 cups flour (part can be wheat flour, bran
   flakes, wheat germ)
2 cups 100% bran
4 eggs

5 teaspoons soda
1 teaspoon salt
1 quart buttermilk
1 pound raisins
4 cups All Bran
2 cups boiling water

Pour boiling water over 100% bran cereal. Cream shortening and sugar. Add beaten eggs and buttermilk. Add both bran cereals. Stir well. Sift flour, soda and salt and add to mixture. Fold in raisins. Bake now or keep in refrigerator for up to 6 weeks, baking as wanted. Bake in a 400° F. oven in greased tins filled ¾ full for 15-18 minutes. Makes 2 quarts muffin mix.

Marvelous way to have "fresh" baked bran muffins every day the easy way! Serve with honey butter and fresh fruit for an easy snack. Approximately 130 calories in each muffin.

Mary Ellen Seitz

Tofu Oat Muffins

1 cup flour
1 cup rolled oats
¼ cup raisins
½ teaspoon salt
1-1½ teaspoons cinnamon
2 teaspoons baking powder

¼ teaspoon baking soda
½ cup sugar
8 ounces (about 1 cup) tofu (soy bean curd)
¼ cup water
2 eggs
¼ cup oil

Mix first 8 ingredients together in a large bowl. Place tofu, water, eggs, and oil in a blender container and blend until smooth. Pour blended ingredients into the flour mixture. Stir well. Fill greased muffin tins ⅔ full. Bake at 425° F. for 12-15 minutes. Makes 12.

High protein muffins and milk free!

Betty R. Worden

37

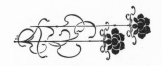

Brunch Ideas

Cheese Strata

5 slices white bread
4 eggs, beaten
2 cups nonfat milk
¾ teaspoon brown sugar
¾ teaspoon Worcestershire sauce

¾ teaspoon seasoned salt
¾ teaspoon dry mustard
Dash white pepper
2½ cups Cheddar cheese, grated

Day before serving, remove crusts and cut bread into cubes. Combine beaten eggs, milk, brown sugar, Worcestershire, salt, dry mustard and pepper. Mix in bread and cheese. Let stand several hours or overnight. Place in a pan of water and bake at 325° F. for 45 minutes. Serve with a cheese sauce, if desired. Serves 6.

This is my daughter's recipe. We use it for Christmas breakfast with fruit and rolls.

Juanita K. Finlayson

Very Popular No Pasta Lasagna

½ cup red wine
5 ripe olives, minced
2 cups tomato juice
1 medium onion, chopped
1 medium green pepper, chopped
1 teaspoon oregano
1 teaspoon basil
1 teaspoon black pepper
2½ cups low fat cottage cheese

½ cup grated Mozzarella cheese (substitute part skim milk Mozzarella cheese)
2 eggs
¼ cup parsley, chopped
½ cup green onion, chopped
1 large eggplant, sliced thin
2-3 zucchini, sliced thin, lengthwise
¼ cup Parmesan cheese

Combine wine, olives, tomato juice, onion, green pepper, oregano, basil and black pepper. Simmer for 2-3 hours to make a sauce. Combine in a separate bowl, cottage cheese, Mozzarella, eggs, parsley and green onion. Use eggplant and zucchini for pasta and layer with sauce and cheese filling. Sprinkle with Parmesan and bake at 350° F. for 1 hour. Serves 6.

157 calories per serving. This is so good—you won't believe it really tastes like lasagna until you have tried it.

Roseanne Bye

Cheese and Chili Casserole

6 eggs
4 tablespoons flour
Salt, pepper to taste
2 cans (13½ ounces each) evaporated skimmed milk

1 pound Jack cheese, grated
1 pound lowfat pasteurized Cheddar cheese, grated
1 can (4 ounce) green chiles, diced (amount depends on preference)

Beat eggs, add flour and mix well. Add evaporated milk, salt and pepper and mix again. The grated cheese may be layered with the chiles or mixed together. Pour

egg mixture over the combined cheeses and chiles. Bake in a greased 9" x 13" baking dish, in a preheated 350° F. oven for 30 minutes or until done in center when tested with a toothpick. Serves 10.

This is one of my favorite brunch recipes for company, especially when served with a fresh fruit compote and bran muffins. It warms up well in a microwave oven.

Barbara Gershman

Tofu Blintzes

Pancake:

1¼ cups buttermilk baking mix
1¾ cups nonfat milk
3 eggs

4 tablespoons butter (optional—best to use non-stick pan)

Filling:

1 pound tofu (soybean curd), drained 30 minutes
1 teaspoon vanilla
1 tablespoon fresh lemon juice
¼ teaspoon salt

½ teaspoon cinnamon
¼ cup sugar (or equivalent amount of sugar substitute)
Sour cream (optional)
Jam (optional)

Beat baking mix, milk and eggs with rotary beater until smooth. Lightly grease skillet with butter as needed to prevent sticking. Spoon about 3 tablespoons batter into hot skillet; spread batter around or tilt pan. Bake on both sides. Makes about 12-15 six-inch pancakes. For filling: mash drained tofu with a fork and add remaining ingredients, except sour cream and jam. Fill pancakes with a rounded tablespoon of tofu mixture and roll up like a jelly roll. Heat in frying pan or in oven 400° F. for 10 minutes. Serve with sour cream and jam if desired. Serves 4.

Lower calories and lower fat than cottage cheese, also less expensive. Try tofu in manicotti or lasagne in place of part of the cheese. Watch sour cream and jam when counting calories.

Betty R. Worden

Potato & Ham Omelette

1 medium onion, finely chopped
2 large potatoes, peeled and sliced
4 tablespoons butter
2 cups chopped ham or procuitto

Salt and pepper
4-5 eggs
Parsley or chives

Heat 2 tablespoons butter in large skillet with sloping sides or an omelet pan. Add onion and potato and cook over very low heat until tender. Add more butter as needed to prevent sticking. Add ham. Sprinkle with salt and pepper and stir thoroughly. Beat eggs until well mixed but be careful not to overbeat them. Pour

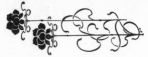

eggs over vegetables and cook on medium heat, lifting edges of omelet to let uncooked portions run underneath. Shake pan during this stage to keep from sticking. When bottom is set, turn and cook. Serves 4-6.

A scrumptious dish for brunch or dinner. Asparagus, rolls and fruit are tasty accompaniments.

Jan Parks

Cottage Cheese Pancakes

1 cup pot cheese or dry curd cottage cheese
½ teaspoon salt
1 tablespoon cornstarch
2 eggs

2 teaspoons honey oil
½ cup applesauce, unsweetened
½ cup lowfat plain yogurt
½ cup fruit or flavored yogurt

Place pot cheese, salt, cornstarch, eggs and honey in the container of an electric blender. Cover and blend at high speed until smooth; stop blender once and push down mixture from sides of container with a spoon. Heat a heavy griddle or skillet over moderately high heat (about 300° F.) and oil very lightly. Drop batter by the tablespoon on the griddle, spreading it slightly with the spoon after dropping. When pancakes are brown on bottom, turn and brown on the other side. Serve with applesauce and yogurt or with fruit flavored yogurt. Makes 16 small pancakes, or 3 servings.

145 calories per serving (without topping). These are moist, delicate, thin, no-flour pancakes. Terrific for brunch!

Joann Driggers

Magical Quiche

½ pound (8 slices) bacon, cooked and crumbled
1 cup Swiss cheese, grated
½ cup fresh onion, finely chopped
1 can (12 ounce) whole kernel corn, drained

2 cups nonfat milk
½ cup buttermilk biscuit mix
4 eggs
¼ teaspoon salt
⅛ teaspoon pepper

Combine and layer: bacon, cheese, onion and corn and spread in a greased 10-inch pan or a deep 10-inch pie pan. Place milk, buttermilk biscuit mix, eggs, salt and pepper in blender. Blend on high speed for 1 minute. Pour over mixture in quiche pan. Bake at 350° F. for 50-55 minutes, or until knife inserted in center comes out clean. Let stand 5 minutes before serving. Serves 4-6.

The corn gives this quiche a different, colorful appeal, and the crust is on top instead of the bottom! Portion control is important in this recipe.

Penny Lewallen

42

Puffed Eggs Monterey

6 eggs
½ cup nonfat milk
1 teaspoon salt
½ teaspoon pepper
2 tablespoons green chiles, chopped

1 cup Jack cheese, grated (substitute part
    skim Mozzarella cheese)
4 slices bread
2 tablespoons butter

Combine eggs, milk, salt, pepper and chiles; beat lightly. Add cheese. Spread bread with butter; cut in half to make triangles. Arrange bread halves, buttered side out, around edge of a 9-inch pie plate so points stand up. Place remaining bread, buttered side down, in bottom of pan. Pour in egg mixture. Bake in 350° F. oven for 30 minutes. Cut into wedges. Serves 4-6.

The triangle points make this an interesting looking brunch idea! Watch portions for low calorie diets.

Carol Heinz-Dooley

Oatmeal Patties

1 cup oatmeal
1 cup lowfat cottage cheese
2 eggs, beaten
1 package onion soup mix

1 teaspoon sage
3 tablespoons wheat germ
1 tablespoon yeast, granular
1 can (10¾ ounce) mushroom soup

Mix all ingredients except mushroom soup. Form into patties and fry. (May be used after this step as burgers on buns and served with catsup, onion slices, pickles etc., if desired or used as entree) Entree: Place patties in baking dish and cover with soup diluted with ½ can water. Bake for 45 minutes at 375° F. Serves 6.

Makes a good substitute for hamburgers when meat is expensive or as an appealing entree for brunch.

Dinah S. Baker R.D.

Acapulco Quiche

3-4 corn tortillas
1 cup milk
6 eggs
½ teaspoon salt
½ teaspoon cumin
1 can (4 ounce) diced green chiles

1 cup Jack cheese, grated
1½ cups Cheddar cheese, grated
Sour cream
Salsa
Guacamole (optional)

Cut tortillas into quarters. Overlap on bottom of 9-inch pie or quiche dish. Place milk in 4-cup measure. Microwave on HIGH for 2 minutes. Add eggs to heated milk. Beat. Add salt, cumin, chiles, Jack cheese and ½ cup of Cheddar cheese. Blend thoroughly. Pour mixture into pie dish (the tortillas may rise). Microwave

43

for 15 minutes on 70% power, turning dish after each 5 minutes. Sprinkle remaining Cheddar cheese on quiche. Microwave for 1-2 minutes on HIGH. Let stand 5-6 minutes. Serve with sour cream, salsa, and guacamole. Serves 4-5.

This can be used as a main dish or as an appetizer.

Mary Ann Sheets

Southwest Quiche

1 9-inch unbaked pie shell
1 tablespoon chile powder
4 eggs, well beaten
1 cup grated Cheddar cheese

1 cup grated Jack cheese
¾ cup half and half
1 can (4 ounce) green chiles, diced
1 can (4 ounce) black olives, chopped

Add chile powder to pie dough before rolling. Mix eggs, cheeses, half and half, green chiles and black olives and pour into the unbaked pie shell. Bake 45 minutes at 400° F. Let stand 5 minutes before slicing. Serves 6.

Excellent brunch idea for those who are lovers of the spicy flavor. Try substituting low fat or non fat milk in the place of the half and half.

Liz Humphrey

Mexicali Souffle

16 slices white bread, crusts trimmed
3 cups Cheddar cheese, grated
6 eggs
3 cups milk
1 teaspoon salt

1 teaspoon pepper
⅓ cup green pepper, chopped
⅓ cup pimiento, chopped
½ teaspoon prepared mustard
4 drops hot pepper sauce

Butter a 9" X 13" baking dish. Place 8 bread slices in bottom of dish. Beat eggs and milk together. Add other ingredients except cheese. Pour half of egg/milk mixture over bread slices. Sprinkle with grated cheese. Place other 8 slices of bread over mixture and repeat process, ending with cheese. Cover with plastic wrap and refrigerate 24 hours. Uncover and bake at 325° F. for 1 hour covered with foil. Remove foil final 15 minutes so top can brown slightly. Let sit a few minutes. Sits very well on warming tray for 15-20 minutes. Serves 8.

A great vegetarian dish and is excellent for brunch!

Karen Lindstrom-Titus

44

Recipe for "Chinese Chicken" on page 64 →

Fancy
CALIFORNIA
FRUITS
WHOLESALE
BLUE ANCHOR, INC.
SACRAMENTO SHIPPERS CALIF. 95813
BLUE ANCHOR, INC.
1912

Chili Cheese Squares

10 eggs
1 pint cottage cheese
½ cup flour
1 teaspoon baking powder
1 teaspoon salt

6 drops bottled, hot pepper sauce
1 pound Jack or Cheddar cheese, cubed
1 can (7 ounce) green chiles, chopped
½ cup butter, melted

Preheat oven to 400° F. In blender whirl ½ of the following: eggs, cottage cheese, flour, baking powder, salt, hot pepper sauce and cheese until blended. Pour into large bowl and repeat with other half of ingredients. Add chiles and butter and mix. Pour into 9" X 13" greased glass baking dish. Bake at 400° F. for 15 minutes. Reduce heat to 350° F. and continue baking for 20-25 minutes until set. Serve warm or cold. Serves 6-8.

Carol Heinz-Dooley

← Recipe for "Virginia's Apple Tart" on page 86

Beef

Beef and Bean Enchilada

1½ pounds round steak, trimmed and
  ground
1 medium onion, chopped
1 can (16 ounce) refried beans
1 teaspoon salt
⅛ teaspoon garlic powder
⅓ cup taco sauce
1 cup ripe olives, quartered and pitted

1 can (10 ounce) enchilada sauce
1 can tomato soup
Salad oil (use sparingly)
12 corn tortillas
3 cups Cheddar cheese, shredded (substitute lowfat pasteurized cheese)
Lowfat plain yogurt

Saute ground beef and onions until meat is browned and onions are soft. Stir in
beans, salt, garlic powder, taco sauce, and olives; heat until bubbly. Combine
enchilada sauce and tomato soup, and heat. Pour half sauce and soup into an
ungreased, shallow 3-quart baking dish. Pour oil to a depth of about ¼-inch in a
small frying pan, and heat. Dip tortillas, one at a time in hot oil; drain quickly and
dip in remaining sauce. Place about ⅓ cup of the bean/beef filling in center of
tortilla. Roll up and place seam side down, in baking dish. Pour remaining sauce
evenly over tortillas, cover with cheese. Bake, uncovered in moderate oven,
350° F. for about 15 minutes or until thoroughly heated. Can be made ahead
and covered and refrigerated for up to 1 day. If taken directly from refrigerator
increase baking time to 45 minutes. Garnish with a dolup of lowfat yogurt and
garnish with olive slices. Chili sauce can be used on top if hotter flavor is
preferred. Serves 6.

*A real hit with men! If you're watching calories closely, limit yourself to a very small
portion.*

Karen Lindstrom-Titus

Beef with Oyster Sauce

1 pound top round steak
½ cup cold water
1 tablespoon cornstarch
2 tablespoons oyster sauce
2 tablespoons dry sherry
1 tablespoon soy sauce
½ teaspoon sugar

2 tablespoons cooking oil
1 bunch green onions, sliced (bias-sliced
  into 1-inch lengths, using some of
  green stems)
½ cup carrots, matchstick size
½ cup zucchini, matchstick size

Partially freeze beef. Slice beef thinly across the grain into bite-size strips. For
marinade, blend water into cornstarch; stir in oyster sauce, sherry, soy sauce, and
sugar; mix well. Add beef; let stand 30 minutes at room temperature. Drain meat,
reserving marinade; set aside. Preheat wok or large skillet over high heat. Add
the oil. Stir-fry onion in hot oil about 3 minutes or until crisp-tender. Remove
onion (add more oil if necessary). Add half the beef to hot wok or skillet; stir fry 2-
3 minutes or until browned. Remove beef. Stir-fry remaining beef 2-3 minutes.
Return all meat to wok or skillet. Stir reserved marinade and stir into beef. Cook

and stir until thickened and bubbly. Stir in onion; cover and cook 1 minute. Serves 4.

Serve at once over hot cooked rice.

Penny Lewallen

Spanish Rice

1 tablespoon shortening
1 pound round steak, trimmed and ground
1 medium onion, diced
1 green pepper, chopped
1 teaspoon salt

1 can (27 ounces) tomatoes
Dash pepper
1 teaspoon prepared mustard
1 teaspoon Worcestershire sauce
1 cup uncooked rice, long grain

Preheat an electric skillet to 350° F. Saute ground meat until brown, remove from pan leaving some fat. Saute onion and pepper in fat and add shortening if necessary. Add remaining ingredients, mix thoroughly. Cover pan. When steaming reduce heat to 200° F. (simmer). Cook 45-60 minutes or until rice is tender. Serves 6.

A good wholesome alternative to hamburger helper! With the addition of rice to this main dish, I only need to serve a tossed salad and nutritious beverage for a complete light meal.

Marilyn Desmond

Green Pepper Steak

¼ cup flour
1 teaspoon salt
¼ teaspoon pepper
2 pounds chuck or round steak, 1-inch
  cubes
¼ cup oil (amount may be reduced to
  eliminate some calories)

2 green peppers, chopped
1 cup celery, chopped
1 cup mushrooms, sliced
2 cloves garlic, mashed
1 cup burgundy wine
1 cup water
¼ cup soy sauce

Place flour, salt, pepper in a plastic bag, add meat and shake to coat. Heat oil in skillet on medium high and brown meat quickly. Add remaining ingredients. Simmer 1½ hours. Serves 6-8.

Serve with tossed salad, steamed rice and a light dessert for raves from your dinner guests.

Virginia Witmer

The Lazy-Lady Swiss

2 pounds round steak
1 scant teaspoon seasoned salt
1 medium onion (or 2 tablespoons dehydrated, minced onion)

1 tablespoon oil
1 cup white wine
1 can (10¾ ounce) cream of mushroom
  soup

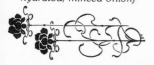

49

Cut steak in narrow strips. Brown in oil on both sides. Chop onion fine or add the dehydrated onion that has been moistened with a little water. Cook until transparent, but not brown. Pour off any excess fat. Salt the steak and add a little pepper if desired. Add wine. Cover and simmer 25-30 minutes or place in the oven at 350° F. for 45 minutes. Add mushroom soup. Bake an additional 45 minutes to an hour. It will have a wonderful sauce of its own. Serves 8.

This recipe is delicious served over poppy seed noodles that have been simmered in canned beef broth and seasoned with just a touch of butter. Make sure the rest of your meal is light with this main dish.

Cadie Mac Lean

Vita Tostada

12 thin corn tortillas, crisped in oven
1 pound ground veal or turkey, cooked
1 cup tomato sauce
2 tablespoons onion, minced
2 teaspoons chili powder
1 teaspoon oregano

¼ teaspoon garlic powder
¼ teaspoon ground black pepper
1 head lettuce, shredded
1 cup tomato, chopped
1 cup sharp Cheddar cheese, grated

Mix together in large frying pan, veal or turkey, tomato sauce, onion, chili powder, oregano, garlic and pepper. Simmer for 5 minutes until heated. Divide among the 12 tortillas. Layer lettuce, tomato and Cheddar cheese on top of meat mixture in the order given. Serves 12.

We really have happy guests when we serve this—so will you! It is yummy. Low in calories if you can enjoy only one.

Roseanne Bye

Oriental-Style Broccoli

½ pound flank steak
1½ pounds broccoli
2 teaspoons Sherry
⅛ teaspoon pepper
2 teaspoons soy sauce

½ teaspoon salt
½ teaspoon sugar
¾ cup water
¼ cup oil
2 teaspoons cornstarch

Put meat in freezer for a few minutes before starting preparation. Cut cold meat across grain into thin slices. Wash broccoli. Cut broccoli flowerettes from stalk. Cut stalks diagonally into ¼-inch slices. Combine Sherry, pepper, soy sauce, salt, sugar, and ½ cup water. Heat 2 tablespoons oil in a heavy skillet or electric skillet set at 360° F. Add broccoli stalk slices. Cover skillet and shake. Cook for 2 minutes. Add flowerettes. Cover and shake another 2 minutes. Check tenderness with fork. Broccoli should be crisp-tender. Place broccoli on hot platter. Place remaining 2 tablespoons oil in hot skillet. Add sliced meat. Brown quickly on both sides. Pour in soy sauce mixture. Cook 2 minutes; covered. Add cooked

broccoli. Dissolve cornstarch in ¼ cup water. Add to broccoli mixture. Stir. Bring to boil. Serves 5-6.

Nice with rice. Pass additional soy sauce. An easy but delicious recipe for those attempting stir-fry cookery for the first time.

Eileen Jo Jackson

Noodle-Cheese Casserole

1 pound lean, ground round
1 onion, chopped
2 cans (8 ounces each) tomato sauce
1 tablespoon sugar
1 carton (8 ounce) sour cream (can sub-
    stitute imitation sour cream)

1 package (3 ounce) cream cheese (sub-
    stitute Neufchatel cheese)
1 package (8 ounce) noodles, cooked
Grated Cheddar cheese (can substitute
    low fat American cheese)

Cook noodles according to package directions. Brown meat and onion in large frying pan. Add tomato sauce and sugar. Cook for 5 minutes. Remove from heat. Add cream cheese and sour cream. Fold into cooked noodles. Top with Cheddar cheese. Bake in casserole at 350° F. for 30-40 minutes. Serves 4-6.

Delicious served with a green salad and apple muffins! To cut more calories from this recipe, try blended cottage cheese instead of the sour cream and use only half the noodles called for in the recipe.

Geraldine MacGill

Tofu Burritos

2 cups frozen tofu (soybean curd), de-
    frosted and crumbled
1 pound round steak, trimmed and ground
    or leftover beef roast
1 medium onion, chopped
2 medium tomatoes, chopped

1 can (8 ounce) green chili salsa
1 can (4 ounce) diced green chiles
1 teaspoon salt
6 large flour tortillas
½ pound cheese, grated

Brown meat in large frypan. Leftover roast may need some oil in the pan to prevent sticking. Add chopped onion and cook until transparent. Drain any fat. Squeeze the tofu to remove excess moisture and crumble. Add to meat with the chili salsa, diced chiles, tomatoes and salt. Stir and cook until most of moisture is gone, about 20 minutes. Serve on a warm tortilla rolled up with some cheese. Serve hot sauce on the side. Makes 6.

Tofu—the nutritious and inexpensive meat extender! High in protein and low in calories!

Betty Worden

51

Rice Pilaf with Meat Balls

1 pound round steak, trimmed and ground
1 pound ground sausage
1 can (5 ounce) water chestnuts, chopped
2 cups chicken broth
2 cups water
1 package (1¾ ounce) dry onion soup mix

1½ cups rice
1 can (16 ounce) bean sprouts, drained or 1 pound fresh Pimiento
Green onion, chopped
2 eggs, scrambled and cut into strips
Soy sauce

Make meat balls by mixing ground beef, sausage and water chestnuts together. Form into 12 balls and bake at 375° F. for 30 minutes. Bring the chicken broth and water to a boil. Add the onion soup and rice and pour mixture into a 2-quart casserole. Cover and bake at 325° F. for 45 minutes or until rice is done. Stir in bean sprouts. Arrange meat balls around top of rice and garnish with green onion, pimiento and egg strips. Serve with soy sauce. Serves 8.

On a round casserole, this looks nice in a pinwheel design. This is a great casserole with an oriental flavor.

Margie Chitwood

Stir Fried Beef, Broccoli and Mushrooms

⅓ cup soy sauce
2 tablespoons cider vinegar
¾ teaspoon sugar
1 beef bouillon cube
⅓ cup water
2 teaspoons cornstarch
3 tablespoons oil
2 large cloves garlic peeled & halved
¾ pound beef (flank or top round), cut in ⅛ diagonal slices

1 large onion peeled, halved and cut into ¼-inch slices (1½ cups)
1½ cups peeled broccoli stems cut into ⅛-inch diagonal slices
2½ cups broccoli flowerettes
¼ pound fresh mushrooms, cut into ⅛-inch slices

Mix soy sauce, vinegar and sugar in a small bowl. In another bowl mix bouillon cube, water and cornstarch. Assemble remaining ingredients. To cook, heat 1½ tablespoons oil over high heat, add garlic and cook. Add meat and stir fry 2 minutes until light brown. Remove meat and juices. Discard garlic. Wipe out wok; add 1 tablespoon oil, when hot add onion and broccoli. Stir fry 2 minutes until tender crisp. Add ½ teaspoon oil and mushrooms. Stir fry 2 minutes, pour in meat and juices. Add soy/vinegar. Stir and cook 2 minutes. Add cornstarch mixture and cook stirring constantly 2 minutes.

Only 294 calories in each serving of the delicious, Oriental-style main dish that has become one of my guests favorites.

Dorothy Wuertz

Beef and Shrimp Kabob

2 pounds beef, round steak or sirloin tip,
    cut in 1½" chunks
1½ pounds medium shrimp, deveined
2 tablespoons honey
1½ cups plain lowfat yogurt
¾ cup chopped onion
1 teaspoon minced garlic
1 small dried hot chili pepper, chopped
¾ teaspoon ground cumin
½ teaspoon nutmeg
¼ teaspoon salt
¼ teaspoon cinnamon

Toss beef and shrimp with all remaining ingredients. Cover and refrigerate overnight. String beef and shrimp on skewers, grill or broil about 15 minutes, turning every 5 minutes. Serves 4-6.

A festive main dish for a summer cook-out. A fresh fruit salad and apple-bran muffins complete the menu.

Carolyn Breeden

Beef Teriyaki

1 pound beef round, cut in julienne strips
¼ cup soy sauce
1 tablespoon dry sherry
1 tablespoon sugar
½ teaspoon ginger
¼ teaspoon garlic powder
Cooked rice (optional)

Cut beef while frozen (⅛-inch thick). In small bowl, mix together soy sauce, sherry, sugar, ginger and garlic powder. Stir in meat and let marinate 10 minutes. Thread on skewers accordian style and broil 4 inches from heat 1-2 minutes on each side or until done as desired. Serve on hot cooked rice. Serves 4-6.

Children enjoy helping "thread" the meat on the sticks. It cooks so quickly that it is a good, last minute meal.

Eileen Jo Jackson

Greek Moussaka

1 pound lean round steak, trimmed and
    ground
2 cups plain tomato sauce
1 small onion, minced
2 teaspoons garlic salt
½ teaspoon dried oregano
⅛ teaspoon cinnamon
⅛ teaspoon ground nutmeg
1 eggplant (about 1¼ pounds) pared and
    diced
2 ounces part-skim feta cheese, crumbled

Break meat into chunks in baking pan and broil until brown. Pour off fat. For sauce, combine tomato sauce, onion, garlic salt, oregano, cinnamon and nutmeg. Layer meat, sauce and eggplant in ovenproof casserole. Sprinkle with cheese. Bake in a preheated 350° F. oven 45 minutes. Serves 4.

A very nutritious and tasty main dish; quite low in calories.

Gretchen Furstenau

Island Teriyaki

½ cup soy sauce
¼ cup brown sugar substitute
2 tablespoons olive oil
1 tablespoon fresh ginger root, grated
½ teaspoon MSG

¼ teaspoon cracked pepper
2 cloves garlic, minced
1½ pounds top sirloin steak, cut in strips
    ¼-inch thick and about 1-inch wide
Canned water chestnuts

In deep bowl, combine all ingredients except meat and chestnuts; mix well. Add meat and stir to coat. Let stand 2 hours at room temperature. Lace meat accordian style on skewers. Add a water chestnut at end of each skewer. Broil over hot coals about 10-12 minutes or to rare, medium rare stage, turning frequently and basting with soy marinade. Serves 4-5.

I usually use a hibachi and let each person cook own meat. Using bamboo skewers is great!

Marlene Himmelberger

Meat Loaf

2 eggs
1 envelope onion soup mix
⅓ cup catsup

¾ cup water
1½ cups bread crumbs
2 pounds round steak, trimmed and ground

Preheat oven to 375° F. In a large mixing bowl, mix eggs, soup mix, catsup, water and bread crumbs. Add the meat and mix well. Put into a bread pan or an 8" x 10" baking dish. Bake 45 minutes or until done.

This is our favorite meat loaf—thanks to onion soup mix! I keep a plastic container of bread crumbs in the freezer so bread crumb recipes are faster. Serves 8.

Norma Takesian

Sweet and Sour Liver

¾ pound calves liver
¼ cup lemon juice
½ onion, cut into chunks
1 tablespoon oil
⅛ teaspoon garlic salt
1 tablespoon soy sauce
1 slice fresh ginger root, peeled, minced

2 packets sugar substitute (.035 ounces
    each) or 1 tablespoon plus 1 teaspoon
    sugar
1 can (8 ounce) pineapple chunks in own
    juice (reserve juice)
½ green pepper, cut into chunks
2 heaping teaspoons cornstarch
Cooked brown or white rice

Cut liver into bite-size pieces. Marinate in lemon juice 1 hour or more. Make sure all pieces are coated. Lightly saute onion in oil. Drain liver and lightly fry with onion. Stir in garlic salt, soy sauce, fresh ginger, artificial sweetener or sugar, pineapple chunks and juice and green pepper. Heat through. Taste and correct seasoning with a little more lemon juice or sugar to achieve desired sweet and

54

sour flavor. Dissolve cornstarch in enough cold water to form a paste. Stir into liver mixture until liquid is thickened and clear. Serve over cooked rice. Serves 2-3.

This is a tasty way to "disguise" liver. Marinating it in lemon juice helps to eliminate the strong flavor.

Barbara Gershman

Muffin Pan Meat Loaves

1 can (8 ounce) tomato sauce	1½ pounds lean ground beef
1 cup fine bread crumbs	¼ cup catsup
1 slightly beaten egg	2 tablespoons brown sugar
1 teaspoon salt	1 tablespoon vinegar
¼ teaspoon pepper	½ teaspoon dry mustard

Combine first 5 ingredients, add ground chuck; mix well and spoon mixture into 18 muffin cups. Combine remaining ingredients; spread over top of meat loaves. Bake at 350° F. for 25 minutes. Serves 6.

Make as above but put in loaf pan and bake at 350° F. for 1 hour.

Penny Lewallen

Bumpy Meatballs

1½ pounds lean ground beef	1 teaspoon Worcestershire sauce
½ cup uncooked, long grain rice	¼ teaspoon pepper
¼ cup water	1 can (10¾ ounce) condensed Cheddar
1 tablespoon instant minced onion (soak	Cheese soup
with 1 tablespoon water for 3 minutes)	¼ cup milk (low fat or non fat may be used)
1 teaspoon salt	Paprika

Mix all ingredients except last three in medium bowl with fork. Shape the mixture with your hands into 20 meatballs. Brown meatballs in skillet over medium heat. Put meatballs in a 1½-quart casserole with cover, ungreased. Heat oven to 350° F. Mix the soup and milk in small bowl until smooth. Pour over the browned meatballs in the casserole. Sprinkle with paprika. Bake for 1 hour or until the rice is tender. Serves 4.

A savory company dish, sure to bring rave notices.

Penny Lewallen

Tamale Pie

1½ pounds lean ground round
1 large onion, chopped
1 green pepper, chopped
1 can (14 ounce) chili beans
1 can (4 ounce) olives, chopped

¾ pound Cheddar cheese, grated (or low
   fat American cheese)
12 corn tortillas
2 cans (8 ounces each) tomato sauce

Brown meat, add chopped onion and green pepper. Add can of chili beans, chopped olives and cheese. Mix together. Spoon mixture on tortillas. Roll loosely. Put in roasting pan, add tomato sauce and 2 cans water. Bake at 300° F. for 1½ hours. Serves 12.

This is a good recipe for potlucks!

Geraldine MacGill

Pork

Macaroni Acapulco

1 pound bulk pork sausage
½ cup onion, chopped
½ cup green pepper, chopped
1 cup canned stewed tomatoes
1 cup buttermilk

1 tablespoon sugar
1 cup elbow macaroni
1½ teaspoons chili powder
½ teaspoon salt

Brown sausage, stirring to keep meat crumbly. Pour off drippings, reserving 2 tablespoons. Saute onion and green pepper in reserved drippings until tender but not browned. Add remaining ingredients; mix well. Cover and simmer 20 minutes, or until macaroni is tender, stirring occasionally. Serves 6.

A quick, popular family dish.

Marian Quire

Cashew Ham and Chicken with Vegetables

1 pound ham steak, trimmed of fat, cut into 1-inch cubes
1 pound chicken fillet (boneless, skinless breasts) cut into 1-inch cubes
1 teaspoon safflower or corn oil
1 cup fat-skimmed chicken broth, canned or homemade
1 package (10 ounce) frozen Italian green beans or whole beans

1½ cups celery, diagonally sliced
1 can (8 ounce) water chestnuts, drained, sliced
2 bell peppers (1 red, 1 green) cut into 1-inch cubes
1 can (4 ounce) sliced mushrooms, drained
1 onion, sliced
1 tablespoon cornstarch
3 tablespoons dry roasted cashews, broken

Spray large nonstick skillet with cooking spray. Combine ham, chicken, and oil in skillet. Cook and stir until lightly browned. Remove from skillet, blot, reserve. Pour off oil from skillet. Combine ¾ cup of the broth with the vegetables in skillet. Simmer covered 5 minutes, stirring occasionally. Mix cornstarch with remaining broth; stir into skillet. Cook and stir until mixture simmers and thickens. Stir in reserved ham and chicken; cook until heated through. Sprinkle with cashews and serve. Serves 8.

A great company dish!

Gretchen Furstenau

Curried Pork Chops

4 loin pork chops, 1-inch thick (use ½-inch thick and cut calories in half)
2 tablespoons flour
1 tablespoon seasoned salt
1½ teaspoons curry powder
¾ teaspoon paprika

½ teaspoon ground black pepper
2 tablespoons cooking oil
¾ cup orange juice
6 whole cloves
¾ teaspoon fresh orange peel
6 thin fresh orange slices

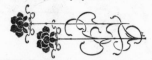
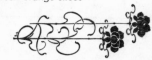

58

Trim excess fat from pork chops. Combine flour and seasonings; reserve 1 tablespoon. Roll chops in remaining mixture until evenly coated. Brown pork chops in oil on Medium-high heat. Reduce the heat to low and add orange juice, cloves, and orange peel. Cover and simmer for 45 minutes, turning occasionally. During last five minutes add orange slices. Remove pork chops and orange slices to a warm platter. Strain remaining liquid; return 1 cup to frypan (add water to make 1 cup if necessary). Combine reserved flour mixture and 2 tablespoons cold water. Pour slowly into liquid and cook on medium until thickened. Spoon sauce over chops. Serves 4.

Sensational taste! Curry and orange mix marvelously.

Carol Heinz-Dooley

Pork Chops Supreme

6 pork chops, ½-inch thick
1 cup hot catsup

6 tablespoons honey
1 large lemon, sliced

Blend catsup and honey and pour over each pork chop. Then top each chop with a slice of fresh lemon. Bake uncovered at 325° F. 1 hour or until done. This same honey sauce is delicious over chicken pieces. Serves 6.

Appeals to men, savory and superb!

Mona Schafer Reed

Jazzed-Up Pork Chops

1 teaspoon oil
6 loin pork chops (may be boned and
  butterflied, but not necessary)
Salt, pepper

2 cups orange juice
½ cup sherry
2 tablespoons dry onion soup mix
1 cup chopped mushrooms

Heat oil in skillet, add pork chops and brown on both sides. Drain off excess fat. (Preceding step may be omitted to eliminate some calories. If this step is being omitted, place pork chops in cold skillet, and proceed.) Sprinkle chops with salt and pepper to taste. Add orange juice, sherry, and soup mix. Cover and simmer 30 minutes. Add mushrooms, cover loosely and simmer 10 minutes longer. The liquid is nearly absorbed during the cooking of the chops and makes a rich sauce. Serve with hot cooked rice, barley, bulgar or wide egg noodles and wilted cabbage, if wanted. Makes 6 servings.

May also be cooked in the microwave oven: 50% power, 16½-18½ minutes to the pound. Liquid will not cook down as much. Cook mushrooms separately for a few minutes (about 2) in a small amount of margarine or butter and add at the end of the cooking time.

Liz Humphrey

Poultry

Easy Chicken Gumbo

2 cups cooked chicken, diced
¼ cup green pepper, chopped
¼ cup onion, chopped
3 tablespoons butter
1 quart chicken broth
1 can (1 pound, 4 ounce) tomatoes
1 bay leaf

1 can (1 pound) cut okra
½ teaspoon salt
⅛ teaspoon pepper
½ teaspoon basil
2 teaspoons sugar
1 tablespoon parsley, minced

Simmer green pepper and onion in butter until soft, stir in chicken broth, tomatoes, bay leaf and okra. Simmer 15 minutes. Remove bay leaf. Add salt, pepper, basil, sugar, parsley, and cooked chicken. Heat thoroughly. Serve with cooked rice. Serves 6.

Recipe served in hunting camp near San Antonio, Texas.

Marlene Himmelberger

Chicken Piquant

4 chicken breasts
¾ cup rosé wine
¼ cup soy sauce
¼ cup salad oil
2 tablespoons water

1 clove garlic, sliced
¼ teaspoon oregano
1 tablespoon brown sugar or brown
  sugar substitute
1 teaspoon ginger

Split 4 chicken breasts in half and place on sides in baking dish. Combine all other ingredients for sauce and pour over chicken breasts. Bake 1½ hours at 375° F. Serve over rice. Serves 4-8.

Marvelous gourmet recipe. I've used it to delight dinner guests often.

Lorraine Nadler

Enchilada Otra Vez (turkey)

1 cup chopped turkey
½ cup chopped onion
½ small can minced chiles (green)
½ pint sour cream (lowfat plain yogurt
  may be used for fewer calories)

1 cup grated Jack or Cheddar cheese
1 small can chopped olives
2 cans enchilada sauce
1 package corn tortillas

Heat tortillas in oil until limp. Remove excess oil. Dip in enchilada sauce. Put spoonful of filling in and roll up. Repeat until tortillas are used up. Pour remainder of sauce over and grate more cheese over the top. Bake in 350° F. oven for 20 minutes. Serves 6-8.

A delightful combination of flavors. This recipe has become a favorite of my family and friends. Limit your servings of this recipe if you are watching calories closely.

Jean Hardy-Hasson

62

Coq Au Vin

1 broiler or roasting chicken
3 tablespoons butter or olive oil
¾ cup mild onion, chopped, or ½ cup
   pearl onions
1 carrot, sliced
3 shallots, minced
1 clove garlic, peeled
2 tablespoons flour
1 tablespoon brandy

2 tablespoons fresh parsley, minced
1 tablespoon fresh chervil or marjoram
½ bay leaf
½ teaspoon thyme
1 teaspoon salt
⅛ teaspoon freshly ground pepper
1½ cups dry red wine or dry sherry
1½ pounds mushrooms sliced

Disjoint the chicken. Melt butter or olive oil. Add and brown lightly, onions, carrot, shallots and garlic. Push the vegetables aside. Brown the chicken in the fat. Add and stir flour, flame with brandy. Add parsley, chervil, bay leaf, thyme, salt and pepper. Stir in wine or sherry. Simmer the chicken over low heat until done, about 1 hour. Keep it covered. Add for the last 5 minutes of cooking, the mushrooms. Skim off excess fat. Correct seasoning. Serve on a hot platter surrounded with sauce and vegetables. Good reheated, actually better. Serves 6-8.

This is wonderful to double for leftovers. It's a lovely country French dinner. You may use white wine instead of red.

Betsy Cook

Chicken Florentine

½ pound fresh spinach, stems removed
1 cup dry lowfat cottage cheese
1 egg
¼ cup Parmesan cheese, grated
1 teaspoon salt
½ teaspoon garlic powder

Dash pepper
4 chicken legs and thighs, joined
2 tablespoons oil
½ teaspoon salt
Pinch each: ground oregano, thyme and
   rosemary

Place spinach with just the water which clings to leaves after washing in a saucepan. Cook until soft and done, about 8 minutes. Cool slightly and squeeze out excess moisture. Chop finely in blender or food processor. Mix cottage cheese, egg, Parmesan cheese, salt, garlic powder and pepper together. Add spinach. Loosen skin on chicken by inserting handle of a teaspoon between skin and meat taking care not to break skin. Stuff pocket formed between skin and meat with the spinach mixture. Place chicken in roasting pan. Brush with oil. Sprinkle with herbs and salt. Roast in 375° F. oven for 45 minutes or until done. Serves 4-6.

This is a different way to combine a vegetable and entree. The spinach mixture is also good when prepared as a separate casserole.

Margie Chitwood

Chinese Chicken

2 teaspoons cornstarch
2 tablespoons soy sauce
1 cup chicken bouillon (2 cubes)
3 chicken breasts, skinned and slivered
4 teaspoons oil for wok
1 green bell pepper, cut in strips
10 mushrooms, sliced

2 stalks celery, sliced
4 green onions, diced
1 can (8 ounce) water chestnuts, drained
  and sliced
1 can (16 ounce) bean sprouts, drained
  or 1 package (6 ounce) frozen Chinese
  pea pods, defrosted

Mix cornstarch with cooled broth and soy sauce until smooth. Stir-fry chicken in wok at 375° F. for 2-3 minutes. Add remaining ingredients and cook until crisp-tender. Add cornstarch mixture, and cook to thicken, about 2 minutes. Serve over rice or noodles. Serves 4-6.

This recipe is a perfect one to change by varying the ingredients. Try adding carrots and "baby" corn-on-the-cob for a new taste treat.

Ruth Jacobson

French Herbed Chicken

4 chicken breast halves
1 tablespoon oil
Salt
Pepper
1 large onion, cut into wedges
½ cup carrot, coarsely chopped
1 clove garlic, crushed
2-3 tablespoons snipped parsley
¼ teaspoon thyme, crushed

⅛ teaspoon marjoram, crushed
⅛ teaspoon sweet basil, crushed
1 medium bay leaf
3 carrots, sliced
2-3 new potatoes cut into ⅛ths
8 mushrooms, sliced
3 pieces of celery with leaves, sliced
1⅔ cups sauterne

Skin chicken and trim off fat. In electric skillet, brown chicken in hot oil. Season with salt and pepper as desired. Add onion and saute lightly. Add all other ingredients, taking care to cover the chicken with the onion pieces, chopped carrot, parsley and crushed herbs. Pour sauterne over all the ingredients. Simmer 45 minutes or until vegetables are done. Add additional water or liquid as needed to retain some liquid in the skillet. Baste the chicken once or twice during the simmering time. Serve with cooking liquid as "gravy." (Can add additional vegetables as desired). Serves 4.

This is one of our favorite chicken dishes. It tastes great reheated, too.

Barbara Gershman

Moo Goo Gai Pan

1 chicken breast
2 teaspoons cornstarch
½ teaspoon salt
¼ teaspoon pepper
1 can (4 ounce) button mushrooms
¼ cup mushroom liquid

1 tablespoon cornstarch
1 garlic clove
3 slices fresh ginger (each the size of a
  nickel)
2 tablespoons oil

64

Skin and bone chicken; then dice. Dredge chicken in cornstarch, salt and pepper. Drain mushrooms, blend liquid from can with remaining cornstarch to a paste. Mince garlic and ginger root. Heat oil. Add garlic and ginger, stir-fry a few minutes. Add chicken and stir-fry until it begins to brown. (2-3 minutes). Add mushrooms; stir-fry only to heat through, then stir in cornstarch paste to thicken. Serve at once. Serves 4.

For color, after browning the chicken, remove chicken, add 1 tablespoon oil and diced green pepper. Stir-fry, add chicken and continue recipe.

Eleanor Widolf

El Pollo Supremo

1 cup tomato juice
1 cup water
2 cups tomato puree
1 cup tomato juice
1 cup water
1 teaspoon salt
½ teaspoon pepper
½ teaspoon baking soda

¼ cup canned green chiles, diced
8 sprigs fresh cilantro, plus more for garnish
1½ pounds skinned, cooked chicken thighs
2 medium green peppers, cut into strips
2 cups fresh mushrooms, sliced
8 ounces onion, cut into eighths and separated

Combine first 10 ingredients in a saucepan. Place over low heat and allow to simmer for 20 minutes. Place chicken thighs in a baking dish. Arrange peppers and mushrooms on top of chicken. Pour sauce mixture evenly over chicken and vegetables. Cover and bake about 30 minutes at 325° F. Divide equally into 4 portions. Garnish each portion with fresh cilantro. Serves 4.

This is good to prepare ahead. All steps except baking can be done the day before. Flavors are blended better the second day. Increase baking time to 40 minutes. Serve as directed.

Roseanne Bye

Paella

1 package of 8 pork link sausage
6 chicken breast halves or assorted pieces
Seasoned salt
Lemon pepper
Garlic powder
1 onion, chopped
2 cans (16 ounce) tomatoes, undrained
2 cups quick brown rice
1 can oysters, drained

1 package (10 ounce) frozen artichoke hearts
6 ounces frozen cooked small shrimp
1 package (10 ounce) frozen peas
Paprika
Parsley flakes or fresh parsley, snipped
1 can (8 ounces) tomato sauce, (optional)

Cut sausages into 1-inch lengths and brown well in electric frypan. Drain and pat well on paper towels. Skin chicken and remove fat. Brown in sausage drippings. Sprinkle with seasoned salt, lemon pepper, garlic powder. Lift out chicken and

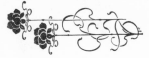

set aside. Saute onion in drippings. When onion is cooked, add tomatoes (break apart) and liquid, rice, oysters, artichoke hearts. Stir together. Stir in cooked sausage pieces and shrimp. Arrange chicken pieces on top. Sprinkle paprika and parsley on chicken. Simmer covered, 30 minutes or until rice is done and moisture is absorbed. Sprinkle on frozen peas toward end of cooking time. (If paella is held on low heat for 30 minutes to 1 hour or more, can add 1 can (8 ounce) tomato sauce to rice and chicken to avoid it drying out). Serves 6-8.

This is a favorite company dish, served with herbed French bread and a large mixed vegetable salad. Limit amount of sausage to cut calories further.

Barbara Gershman

Chinese Noodle Casserole

2 cans (10¾ ounce each) celery soup
3 small cans chicken, or 3-4 chicken
   breasts
1 package slivered almonds
1 can water chestnuts
¾ can (medium size) evaporated milk

3 cans dry Chinese noodles
1 can bean sprouts
1 tablespoon Worcestershire sauce
1 jar mushrooms, or use fresh
1 medium onion, chopped fine

Drain all the juices off the cans of ingredients. Put in large mixing bowl and mix all but the dry noodles together. Spread 1½ cans dry noodles on bottom of 9" X 15" glass baking dish. Spread mixture over the noodles and top with the rest of the dry noodles. If you use the chicken breasts, the broth gives added flavor. Then cut down a little on the milk, but if it cooks too dry add more milk. Bake at 325° F. for 1 hour. Serves 6.

Great with a tropical fruit salad.

Milly Powell

Chicken Parmesan

2 cups fine dry bread crumbs
¾ cup Parmesan cheese
1 teaspoon monosodium glutamate
1 teaspoon paprika
¼ cup minced parsley
1 teaspoon oregano

¼ teaspoon basil
2 teaspoons salt
⅛ teaspoon pepper
2 broiler-fryers, cut-up, or chicken pieces
   of your choice
¾ cup margarine, melted

Mix bread crumbs, cheese, MSG, paprika, parsley, oregano, basil, salt and pepper. Dip chicken pieces in melted margarine, then roll in bread crumb mixture until well coated. Arrange pieces skin-side up in a foil lined shallow baking pan. Bake at 375° F. for 1 hour or until tender. Do not turn chicken pieces while baking. Serves 8.

66

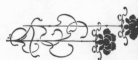

The aroma while cooking is as terrific as the actual taste. Crumb mixture can be made up in quantity and kept in the freezer for quick use.

Delicious flavor! I've substituted tomato juice for the margarine and the flavor is great . . . fewer calories, too!

Eileen Jo Jackson

Chicken Divan Crepes

¼ cup butter
¼ cup flour
2 cups chicken broth
2 teaspoons Worcestershire sauce
3 cups Cheddar cheese, grated
2 cups sour cream

2 packages (10 ounces each) frozen
    broccoli spears or 1½ pounds fresh,
    cooked and drained
2 cups cooked chicken
12 cooked crepes

Over medium heat, melt butter in small saucepan. Stir in flour and cook until bubbly. Add broth and Worcestershire sauce; cook, stirring until thickened. Add 2 cups cheese. Empty sour cream into medium bowl; gradually add hot cheese sauce stirring constantly. In large shallow baking dish, place cooked broccoli and cooked chicken on each crepe. Spoon 1 tablespoon sauce over each. Fold crepes over. Pour remaining sauce over all. Sprinkle with remaining cheese. Cover and heat in 350° F. oven for 20-30 minutes. Makes 12.

Serve with melon salad. Fool-proof enough to try on company.

Nancy Bryant

Seafood

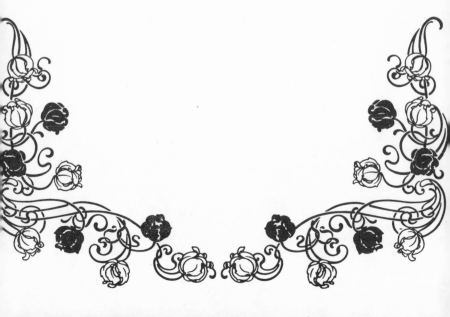

Seviche

2 pounds white fish (Turbot or white
  Islandic halibut)
1 can (29 ounce) tomatoes, mashed
3 ounces stuffed green olives, diced
½ cup catsup
⅓ cup vinegar

1 medium onion, diced
1 teaspoon dried oregano
¼ cup olive oil
10 drops (or more) hot pepper sauce
1 teaspoon salt
Lime juice

Cube the fish into ½-inch squares, put into bowl and cover with 8 ounces lime juice overnight. Rinse off juice in the morning. Add tomatoes, green olives, catsup, vinegar, onion, oregano, olive oil, hot pepper sauce and salt. Chill 2 hours. Serve on avocado halves, garnish with lemon juice. Serves 10.

This recipe came from a famous Laguna Niguel caterer.

Nancy Bryant

Stir Fried Spicy Shrimps

½-¾ pound raw shrimp, shelled and
  deveined
½ teaspoon salt
2 teaspoons cornstarch
2 teaspoons sherry
1 medium bunch broccoli, flowers only
2 large stalks green onions, chopped
4 very thin slices ginger, minced
3 cloves garlic, chopped

1-2 teaspoons Chinese chili sauce (or
  more if you like it very spicy)
Salt (⅛ teaspoon or more to your taste)
½ cup catsup
½ cup water
3 tablespoons sugar
1 teaspoon sesame oil
Oil for cooking (2-3 tablespoons)

Heat 1 tablespoon oil in wok, stir fry broccoli just until heated through, season with a little salt. Remove to serving plate. Keep warm. Heat additional oil in the same wok (1-2 tablespoons), add in garlic and ginger, stir fry until fragrant, add in shrimp, continue stir frying until shrimp turn pinkish in color, add in chili sauce, stir fry until blended in, add in seasoning sauce and chopped green onions, cook for another minute. Stir fry well to assure blending of flavors. Arrange broccoli and shrimp on same serving plate. Serve hot. Serves 4.

Betty Ku

Scallops French Style

1½ pounds scallops, medium size
2 tablespoons fresh lemon juice
4 tablespoons diet margarine
2 cloves garlic, crushed
2 shallots or green onions, minced
3 medium tomatoes, peeled and chopped

½ cup dry white wine
¼ teaspoon salt
¼ teaspoon pepper
Fresh chopped parsley
Freshly grated Parmesan cheese

Marinate scallops in lemon juice for 15 minutes. Drain, pat dry and halve. In large skillet, sauté scallops in melted diet margarine until brown. Don't

overcrowd. Should take about 2 minutes per side. Remove scallops and set aside. Add to skillet: garlic, shallots, tomatoes, wine, salt and pepper. Cook uncovered for 15 minutes. Stir occasionally. Return scallops to skillet. Cook 5 minutes longer, shaking skillet to prevent sticking. Serve in heated scallop shells. Top with Parmesan cheese and chopped parsley. Serves 6-8 as main course. Serves 10 as first course.

Friends who are watching their weight always enjoy this dish!

Susie Pendleton

Light Seafood Spaghetti

8-16 ounces Linguini, spaghetti, or other
    thin pasta
½ cup or 1 cube butter
2 cloves garlic, crushed
½ cup chopped green onion (optional)
1-1½ cups finely cut parsley
2 tablespoons olive oil
2 pounds shark steaks, cut in 1-inch
    cubes or other fresh fish (canned tuna
    may be used in an emergency to stretch
    dish)
2 pounds fresh or frozen squid, cleaned,
    skinned (body tube part cut into ½-
    inch rings) (tentacles may also be used)

Other seafood (optional) shrimp, clams,
    other fish, left-over fish
¼ cup lemon juice
1 tablespoon lemon rind, grated
⅓-½ cup dry vermouth or more
1 red bell pepper, roasted, peeled, seeded
    and sliced into strips
8 ounces natural cured black olives, Italian
    or Greek
Salt and pepper to taste
Grated Parmesan or Romano cheese

Set out all ingredients before cooking. Cooking time is very short and the instant cooking is the secret of good Calamari (squid) even more critical than other fish. Prepare pasta by bringing to a rolling boil, a large pot of water with 1 teaspoon of olive oil in it. Add pasta and simmer according to directions on package or until cooked. Drain in colander in sink and rinse with hot water. Return to pot with tight lid and hold. In skillet saute in half of butter, garlic, parsley, onion. Set aside in large bowl. Saute in other half of butter, shark or other fresh fish. Add vermouth, seasonings, lemon juice, rind, olives, red peppers. Set aside with garlic and parsley mixture. Saute instantly in olive oil, add squid, only until edges begin to curl slightly. Add the other pre-cooked ingredients. Season to taste. Add more butter and vermouth if desired to stretch sauce. Serve over prepared hot pasta. Sprinkle with grated Parmesan or Romano cheese. Serves 8-10.

Many variations are possible from the basic parsley-butter-vermouth sauce. It's different. I serve this to my Epicurean friends. Preparing squid the first time is a challenge. After you get the hang of it—you'll be hooked on how wonderful only YOU can prepare it!

Victoria Anderson

71

Tasty Turbot

1-2 teaspoons butter
½ pound turbot
1-2 Spring onions, chopped

2 bay leaves
Paprika

Melt butter in non-stick fry pan. Place fish in pan. Cook on medium-high heat for 2 minutes. On top of fish, sprinkle onions and crushed bay leaves. Sprinkle lightly with paprika for color. Cook on medium-low heat 9 minutes. Serve with green or spinach salad. Great for lunch or light dinner. Serves 2.

Very fast, very simple and very good.

Jeannie Foley

Scallops Supreme

1 pound fresh or frozen scallops
Salt and pepper, as desired
Juice of ½ lemon

3 strips bacon
1 egg

Rinse 1 pound of fresh or frozen scallops and dry on paper towels. Lightly coat bottom of a shallow 8-inch or 9-inch pan with oil. Place scallops in pan and season with salt, pepper, and juice of ½ lemon. Lay 3 bacon strips over scallops. Broil under low broiler heat until scallops and bacon are done. Don't overcook. When the bacon is done the scallops will be, also. They may be served as is, but the following delicious sauce adds a gourmet touch. Put the scallops and bacon on slices of toast. Stir a slightly beaten egg into the juices in the pan. Stir over moderate surface heat until slightly thickened. Pour over scallops. Serves 2-4.

Low in calories and delicious!

Kathleen Reynolds

Halibut Ragout

½ cup chopped onion
1 clove garlic, minced
½ cup chopped green pepper
3 stalks celery, sliced diagonally
3-4 carrots, sliced
2 tablespoons oil
2 cans (16 ounces each) tomatoes
1 cup water

2 chicken bouillon cubes
2 pounds halibut (cut in cubes)
3 tablespoons minced parsley
1 teaspoon salt
⅛ teaspoon pepper
¼ teaspoon thyme
¼ teaspoon basil

Cook onion, garlic, green pepper, celery and carrots in oil for a few minutes. Add tomatoes, water, bouillon and seasonings. Cover and simmer 20 minutes. Add halibut. Cover and cook 5-10 minutes longer. Sprinkle with parsley. Serves 6.

A long-time favorite and low in calories!

Jeanne Dorse-Smith

Seafood Chowder

1 medium onion, finely chopped
3 ribs celery, finely chopped
1 clove garlic pressed
¼ cup butter
½ cup dry white wine
1 tablespoon chicken base
1 tablespoon salt
½ teaspoon thyme
½ teaspoon nutmeg
½ teaspoon pepper
1 bay leaf

5 tablespoons flour
¼ cup cold water
1 pound fish fillets, cut in cubes (firm
   white fish)
10 ounces oysters, drained; reserve liquid
1 can minced clams, drained; reserve liquid
1 can tiny shrimp, drained; reserve liquid
1 cup evaporated skim milk
Chopped parsley
1½ cups small shell macaroni

In a large heavy casserole, melt butter and when foaming subsides, add onion, celery and garlic. Cook, stirring frequently, 5-8 minutes until soft but not brown. Combine the reserved liquid from oysters, clams and shrimp and add enough water to measure 3 cups. Add to sauteed mixture. Add bay leaf, seasonings, chicken base and wine. Blend flour and water and add stirring constantly. Cook until smooth and thickened. Add fish and oysters. Simmer about 10 minutes. Cook the macaroni shells in 2 quarts boiling salted water until tender, about 8 minutes. Remove bay leaf and add macaroni, milk, clams and shrimp. Heat to simmer. Add salt if necessary. Garnish with chopped parsley. Lobsters, scallops or salmon may be substituted. The use of fresh fish fillets and oysters are recommended. Serves 8.

This is a luxurious chowder, the queen/king of chowders.

Maureen Ramer

73

Vegetables and Accompaniments

Armenian Style Eggplant

1 eggplant (do not peel)
1½ cups Jack cheese, grated
1 egg
½ cup parsley, chopped

Butter (use sparingly)
Salt and pepper
Slices of tomato

Slice the eggplant ½-inch thick. Place slices on buttered cookie sheet. Lightly butter and salt and pepper. Combine the grated cheese, chopped parsley with egg; spread some of mixture on each slice of eggplant. Then top each slice with a slice of tomato, a dab of butter and salt and pepper to taste. Bake at 350° F. for about 45 minutes or until eggplant is tender. The amount of cheese-parsley mixture varies with the size of the eggplant. Sometimes I add 2 eggs to the mixture for creamy consistency. Serves 6-8.

An attractive and different way to serve eggplant—one everyone likes!

Norma Takesian

Zucchini Frittata

1 cup thinly sliced onion
3½ cups (3 medium) zucchini, cut in ⅛-
  inch slices
¼ cup (1 ounce) Italian salami, diced
½ teaspoon salt
2 tablespoons olive oil

5 eggs
½ cup Parmesan cheese, grated
½ cup nonfat milk
½ teaspoon basil leaves, crushed
⅛ teaspoon pepper
1 tablespoon butter

Saute onion, zucchini, salami, and salt in oil in oven-proof 10-inch skillet until zucchini is crisp-tender. Cool slightly. Beat eggs in medium bowl until blended. Add Parmesan cheese, milk, basil, and pepper; beat thoroughly. Add cooked vegetables to egg mixture; stir to combine. Melt butter in same skillet; carefully pour in egg-vegetable mixture. Bake in slow oven, 325° F. 15-20 minutes or until eggs are set. Cut into wedges; serve immediately.

MICROWAVE METHOD: Combine onion, zucchini, salami, salt and oil in 2-quart casserole dish. Micro on HIGH 12 minutes, stirring every 6 minutes. Stir in 1 tablespoon butter. Beat eggs in medium bowl until blended. Add Parmesan cheese, milk, basil, and pepper; beat thoroughly. Add egg mixture to cooked vegetables; stir to combine. Micro on HIGH 4 minutes; rotate ½ turn. Micro on MEDIUM 8 minutes; rotate ¼ turn every 2 minutes. Remove from oven; let stand 5 minutes. Serve. Serves 4.

A tasty, nutritional, easy appetizer, main dish, snack or even brunch dish.

Mary McMurrin

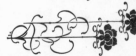

Brussels Sprouts, California Style

½ cup celery, sliced
¼ cup onion, sliced
2 tablespoons olive oil (may use salad oil)
2 packages (10 ounce) frozen Brussels
  sprouts, partially thawed

1 can (8 ounce) stewed tomatoes
¾ teaspoon salt
¼ teaspoon oregano leaves
Dash pepper

In skillet: saute celery and onion in oil; add remaining ingredients. Cover and simmer 5-7 minutes until Brussels sprouts are tender. Serves 6.

A nice way to "jazz" up Brussels sprouts—added flavor and added color!

Eileen Jo Jackson

Aunt Fanny's Baked Squash

3 pounds yellow summer squash
½ cup onions, chopped
½ cup cracker meal or bread crumbs
2 eggs

½ cup diet margarine
1 tablespoon sugar
1 teaspoon salt
½ teaspoon black pepper

Wash and slice squash. Boil until tender; drain thoroughly, then mash. Add all ingredients except ½ of butter and cracker meal to squash. Melt remaining butter. Pour squash mixture in baking dish, then spread butter over top and sprinkle with cracker meal or bread crumbs. Bake in 375° F. oven for approximately 1 hour, or until brown on top. Serves 8-10.

Famous squash dish served at restaurant "Aunt Fanny's Cabin" in Smyrna, Georgia.

Marlene Himmelberger

Eggplant Casserole

1 egg, beaten slightly
1 cup dry bread crumbs
1 medium eggplant, sliced into half-inch
  thick slices
1 cup onion, chopped

1 cup green pepper, chopped
1 can (10 ounce) tomato soup
¼ cup water
1 cup cheese, grated

Dip sliced eggplant in beaten egg and then in crumbs. Fry in oil until partially cooked. Arrange in buttered casserole in alternate layers with onion and pepper mixture. Mix tomato soup with water and pour over eggplant. Sprinkle with cheese. Bake at 350° F. for 35 minutes. Serves 6.

Eggplant will become your favorite vegetable if you serve it like this!

Dinah Baker

77

Spinach Continental

2 packages (10 ounce) frozen chopped
   spinach
1 can (4 ounces) mushroom stems and
   pieces, drained (reserve liquid)
1 can (8½ ounce) water chestnuts, drained
   and sliced
2 teaspoons salt
2 teaspoons instant minced onion
¼ teaspoon garlic powder
1 cup unflavored lowfat yogurt

Cook spinach as directed on package *except* use reserved mushroom liquid and enough water (not salted) to measure ½ cup; drain. Stir in remaining ingredients. Heat over low flame, stirring occasionally, just until mixture simmers. Serves 6 at ⅔ cups each.

A new delicious way with spinach. Everyone will ask for seconds.

Carol Heinz-Dooley

Pesto-Stuffed Tomatoes

8 medium tomatoes (about 2¾ pounds)
1 package (10 ounce) frozen peas, completely thawed
⅔ cup Parmesan cheese, grated
⅓ cup butter or margarine, melted
¼ cup parsley sprigs, packed
1 tablespoon basil, crushed
1 clove garlic, crushed
¼ cup walnuts, finely chopped

Core tomatoes, scoop out insides, chop pulp and set aside. Discard seeds, drain tomatoes on paper towels. Combine peas, cheese, butter, parsley, basil and garlic in food processor or blender container. Cover and blend until smooth. Fold in chopped tomato pulp and walnuts. Place tomato shells in shallow baking pan. Spoon pea mixture into shells, sprinkle with additional Parmesan cheese, if desired. Bake at 350° F. 20-25 minutes. Serves 8.

This is a very pretty vegetable dish. A complete meal would consist of Pesto-Stuffed Tomatoes, pasta, salad, vino, fresh fruit.

Phyllis Specht

Artichoke Souffle

2 jars (6 ounce each) artichoke hearts,
   chopped
1 small onion, chopped
1 clove garlic, minced
4 eggs
¼ cup bread crumbs
¼ teaspoon salt
⅛ teaspoon pepper
⅛ teaspoon bottled hot pepper sauce
⅛ teaspoon oregano
½ pound Cheddar cheese, grated
2 tablespoons parsley, minced

Saute onion and garlic in the marinade from one jar of the artichoke hearts. Beat
eggs with fork. Add crumbs, salt, pepper, oregano and hot pepper sauce. Stir in

78

cheese, parsley, artichoke hearts and sauteed mixture. Pour into a 9-inch square pan. Bake 30 minutes in 325° F. oven. Serves 9.

A glamorous vegetable dish to accompany a meat main dish. Keep portions small.

Alta Gruenwald

Broccoli Custard

2 pounds broccoli, cut in 2-inch pieces
4 eggs, beaten
2 cups lowfat cottage cheese
1 can (8 ounce) whole kernel corn
⅓ cup green onion, chopped
1 cup Cheddar cheese, grated (substitute
    part lowfat cheese)

Dash hot pepper sauce
Salt and pepper to taste
¼ cup butter or margarine
⅔ cup seasoned bread crumbs

Place broccoli in a greased 11" x 8" x 2" dish. Combine eggs and cottage cheese in large bowl and mix well. Add drained corn, onion, cheese, hot pepper sauce, salt and pepper. Pour over broccoli. Melt butter and combine with bread crumbs. Sprinkle over top of casserole and bake at 325° F. 45 minutes. Cool 5 minutes before serving. Serves 6-8.

Serve with green salad and hot rolls and you have a complete meal!

Shelly J. Wellins

Zucchini Casserole

3 large zucchini, washed
2 cups water
2 eggs
1 cup mayonnaise or salad dressing
1 medium onion, chopped
¼ cup green pepper, chopped

1 teaspoon salt
¼ teaspoon pepper
1 cup Parmesan cheese, grated
1 cup soft white bread crumbs (2 slices)
2 tablespoons butter or margarine

Trim zucchini and cut into thin slices. Cook in water in large saucepan 5 minutes, or until tender-crisp. Drain. While zucchini cooks, beat eggs until foamy in large bowl. Stir in mayonnaise or salad dressing, onion, green pepper, salt and pepper. Add drained zucchini and Parmesan cheese and stir until well blended. Pour into 6 cup shallow casserole. Sprinkle with crumbs and dot with butter. Bake at 350° F. for 30 minutes or until golden. Serves 6.

Yellow crookneck squash are also good in this recipe. Remember, salad dressing is high in calories—enjoy small portions.

Nancy Hufstetler

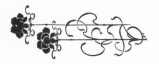

79

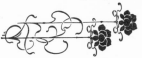

Sherried Sweet Potatoes

7 sweet potatoes or yams
¼ cup diet margarine
¼-½ cup packed brown sugar substitute

¼ cup cream sherry
1 teaspoon salt
Dash pepper

Heat sweet potatoes and enough water to cover, to boiling. Reduce heat to low; cover and simmer 30-40 minutes until fork tender, drain and peel. In large bowl with mixer at low speed, beat sweet potatoes and margarine until smooth, scraping bowl constantly with rubber spatula. Add brown sugar, sherry, salt and pepper. Increase speed to medium; beat 2 minutes longer or until mixture is light and fluffy. Serves 8.

A favorite of non sweet potatoes lovers!

Karen Lindstrom-Titus

Asparagus Chinese Style

2 pounds fresh asparagus
2 tablespoons olive oil or salad oil
¾ cup chicken stock
1 tablespoon cornstarch

2 tablespoons soy sauce
1 tablespoon cold water
1 clove garlic, minced or mashed
Salt and pepper to taste

Wash asparagus well and snap off lower stalks. Cut diagonally in very thin slices. Saute sliced asparagus in hot oil on medium heat for 2 minutes. Remove from heat. Bring chicken stock to boiling point on high heat then turn to low and stir in a mixture of cornstarch, water and soy sauce; stirring constantly. Cook until thickened. Add garlic, salt and pepper to taste. Add asparagus to sauce, cook 1 minute longer stirring constantly. Serve at once. Serves 6.

Broccoli or other vegetables can be used by changing the time.

Carol Heinz-Dooley

Chinese Broccoli

1 pound fresh broccoli
2 tablespoons soy sauce
2 tablespoons oil

2 tablespoons water
½ teaspoon sugar

Clean broccoli. Cut into diagonal slices. Boil broccoli in salted water for 5 minutes. (put stems in water and let cook until boiling, then add tops.) Cover for first 2 minutes and leave uncovered for 3 minutes. Drain. Rinse with cold water. Drain. Keep on hot tray in pan. Before serving, pour hot oil on broccoli. Heat soy sauce, water and sugar. Put broccoli in serving dish. Pour soy sauce mixture over broccoli. Serves 4.

Especially good with simple meat dishes.

Penny Lewallen

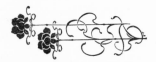

Mina's Sugar Free Cranberry Relish

1 package (12 ounce) cranberries
1 navel orange, cut into eighths
1 red delicious apple, cut into eighths
1 ripe persimmon

½ cup walnuts, chopped
3 tablespoons brown sugar substitute
Few drops red food color, if desired

Put persimmon, cranberries, apple and orange in food processor and chop by pulsing on and off. Add walnuts and brown sugar twin. Mix and store in refrigerator. Serves 4-6.

Better if it stands overnight in refrigerator. Keeps well.

Mina Harper Hutchinson

Calorie Counter's Potato Casserole

3 medium potatoes, pared and cubed
Water
1½ teaspoons salt, divided
1½ cups lowfat cottage cheese
¼ cup skim milk

1 tablespoon lemon juice
½ teaspoon salt
⅛ teaspoon pepper
¼ teaspoon dried dill
2 tablespoons bread crumbs

In a medium saucepan, combine potatoes with 1-inch of cold water and 1 teaspoon salt. Bring to a boil, cover, reduce heat, simmer 15-20 minutes, until potatoes are just tender. Drain, place potatoes in a 1½-quart casserole; set aside. In container of electric blender or food processor, combine cottage cheese, milk, lemon juice, remaining salt, pepper and dill; process until smooth. Pour sauce over potatoes, toss to coat evenly. Sprinkle with bread crumbs. Bake in a 350° F. oven 15-20 minutes or until heated through. This can be made ahead and refrigerated and then back in oven 45 minutes to an hour. Serves 6.

93 calories per serving. Excellent vegetable dish for those who are watching the calories!

Alta Gruenwald

Stir-Fried Yellow Squash (Chinese)

2 tablespoons oil
1 green onion
1 pound yellow squash

1 teaspoon salt
½ teaspoon sugar
2 tablespoons water

Peel and cut squash into ½-inch strips, slice each strip into ¼-inch slices. Chop the onion and stir-fry it in the oil for a few seconds. Add squash, cook and stir 1 minute. Add seasonings and water, cover and cook 3 minutes. Serves 4.

With this recipe, people who don't like squash change their minds. You don't need a wok; a flat heavy frying pan works just as well!

Eleanor Widolf

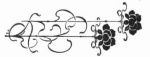

Baked Stuffed Potatoes

3 whole potatoes
⅓ cup chopped onions, water sauteed
1 egg white, stiffly beaten
1 cup nonfat buttermilk
⅛-¼ teaspoon prepared mustard
½-1½ teaspoon dried or fresh parsley

⅛-¼ teaspoon dillweed
½ teaspoon onion powder
½ teaspoon garlic powder
¼ teaspoon horseradish (optional)
¼-½ teaspoon paprika

Wash the potatoes thoroughly and bake them in a 350° F. oven for 1-1½ hours, or until tender. Cut the potatoes in half lengthwise and scoop out the insides with a spoon. Save the skins for stuffing. Whip potatoes with the mustard, other seasonings, and buttermilk. Fold in the egg whites last. Stuff the potato skins with the mashed potatoes and lay them in nonstick baking pans. Sprinkle with paprika and parsley and bake in a 350° F. oven until hot and browned. Serves 6.

A new way to prepare a much-used vegetable. Delicious and nutritious!

Karin Haydt

Zesty Zucchini

1 pound zucchini
⅓ cup low-calorie zesty Italian salad
  dressing

2 tablespoons Parmesan cheese

Wash zucchini and cut into diagonal slices, oriental style. Place salad dressing and zucchini in saute pan. Cook until tender, about 5 minutes. Sprinkle cheese over top and serve.

This is a really quick and delicious vegetable dish which compliments most main dishes.

Margie Chitwood

Orange Rice

2 cups water
2 tablespoons grated orange peel
½ cup orange juice

½ teaspoon salt
1 cup uncooked, long-grain rice
½ cup currants or raisins

Combine water, orange peel, orange juice and salt and bring to a boil. Stir in rice and currants. Return to boiling. Lower heat, cover and cook over low heat until rice is tender and liquid is absorbed (about 25 minutes). Serve hot. Makes 7 half cup servings.

This is especially good when served with shrimp or turkey curry.

Barbara Gershman

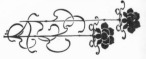

Treasured Carrot Coins

6 medium carrots
2 tablespoons margarine
3 tablespoons water
½ teaspoon salt
1 tablespoon honey

1 tablespoon cream or undiluted skimmed
   evaporated milk
2 teaspoons fresh or freeze-dried, chopped
   parsley

Pare carrots. Slice into thin rounds. Place in skillet with margarine, water, and salt. Cover tightly and simmer 15-20 minutes, or until carrots are barely tender. Add honey, cream and parsley; simmer uncovered 2 minutes longer. Serves 4-5.

Attractive and delicious. Even children like carrots when prepared in this manner.

Eileen Jo Jackson

Carrot-Onion Casserole

2 pound package frozen crinkle cut
   carrots
2 chicken bouillon cubes

½ cup water
3-4 medium onions, sliced
½ cup butter

Dissolve chicken bouillon cubes in ½-¾ cup water. Add frozen carrots and cook covered 10 minutes. Melt ½ cup butter in large skillet and add onion slices. Cook covered about 15 minutes, stirring occasionally. Stir in 1 tablespoon flour, ¼ teaspoon salt, pepper and ¾ cup water. Add carrots with liquid and pinch of sugar. Simmer uncovered 5 minutes. Serve, or put in casserole for re-heating later. Serves 8.

Great make ahead vegetable!

Norma Takesian

Zucchini Ricotta Bake

2 medium zucchini
⅓ cup part skim Ricotta cheese
1 ounce part skim Mozzarella cheese,
   grated

½ cup tomato puree
Italian seasoning, garlic powder, and
   onion salt to taste

In a saucepan simmer zucchini in water until tender crisp. Cut zucchini in half. Remove insides and mix with Ricotta cheese. Fill zucchini shells with Ricotta mixture. Place filled shells in a baking dish. In a bowl combine puree and seasonings and pour over zucchini. Sprinkle Mozzarella on top. Bake at 350° F. 15 minutes or until heated through. Serves 1 for lunch.

If you like zucchini and Italian style foods in general, you will love this dish!

Roseanne Bye

Desserts

Budino di Ricotta (Ricotta Soufflé)

15 ounces part skim Ricotta or lowfat
   cottage cheese
1 orange

4 eggs
2 tablespoons all-purpose flour
11 tablespoons granulated sugar

Place Ricotta in bowl. Grate orange peel into Ricotta. Separate 3 of the eggs and add the yolks and the remaining whole egg and mix thoroughly, with Ricotta. When mixture is smooth, add flour, and 7 tablespoons sugar. Beat the 3 egg whites until stiff and gently fold into the Ricotta mixture. Butter a soufflé dish, 8½ inches in diameter, and coat it with the remaining sugar. Pour soufflé mixture into prepared dish and place in preheated oven (375° F) for 45 minutes. Serves 6.

A lovely light dessert to end any luncheon or dinner party.

Phyllis Specht

Winners Squash Pie

1 pound yellow squash
¼ cup honey
1 tablespoon molasses

¼ teaspoon each ginger and allspice
2 teaspoons cinnamon
2 eggs

Steam squash until tender. Cool and place in blender. Add to squash: honey, molasses, ginger, allspice, cinnamon, and eggs. Blend well. Sprinkle with nutmeg. Bake in large square pans at 325° F. for 1 hour. Serves 12.

75 calories per serving, or try 25 servings at 37 calories each! Tastes like pumpkin pie, looks like pumpkin. Our guests love it and never miss the crust.

Roseanne Bye

Virginia's Apple Tart

½ cup unsweetened apple juice
¼ teaspoon maple extract
¼ teaspoon cinnamon, ground
2 teaspoons fructose

½ teaspoon cornstarch
3 medium tart apples, cored and thinly
   sliced
Apple Tart Crust

In a saucepan, combine apple juice, maple extract, cinnamon, fructose, and cornstarch. Stir until blended. Cook and stir over low heat until thickened and smooth. Remove from heat, add sliced apples, and stir to coat apple slices well. Turn into pie crust, arranging apple slices pinwheel fashion. Bake at 425° for 20 to 30 minutes, or until apples are tender and crust is browned. Serves 8.

Apple Tart Crust

¾ cup flour
¼ teaspoon lemon peel, grated
¼ teaspoon orange peel, grated

3 tablespoons vegetable oil
1½ tablespoons nonfat milk

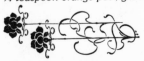

Combine flour and lemon and orange peels in a small mixing bowl. Combine oil and milk in a measuring cup, but do not stir. Add all at once to flour mixture. Mix quickly with a fork until flour mixture begins to form a ball. Roll out between sheets of waxed paper to a very thin 12-inch circle. Fit over an 8 or 9-inch pie plate or tart pan, trimming edges. Dough may be chilled at this point. Pierce dough with a fork in several places to allow steam to escape during baking. Bake at 450° for 5 minutes or until golden. Cool before filling.

Pretty and fun to serve to guests. Looks like more than the 125 calories per serving.

Virginia Witmer

Lemon Pineapple Mousse

1 box (½ ounce) dietary lemon gelatin
    dessert
2 cups boiling water

1 pint pineapple sherbet
1 tablespoon lemon juice
1 tablespoon lemon rind, grated

Dissolve gelatin in boiling water. Add sherbet, lemon juice and lemon rind. Beat on low speed of electric mixer until sherbet is melted. Divide into 6 sherbet dishes. Chill until set. Serves 6.

A light dessert at 80 calories per serving!

Carol Heinz-Dooley

Apple Dump Cake

1 can sliced apples (not apple pie filling)
2 eggs
2 cups sugar
½ cup oil
1 teaspoon cinnamon

1 teaspoon vanilla
1 teaspoon salt
2 teaspoons soda
1 cup nuts, chopped
2 cups flour

Mix all ingredients together. "Dump" into a greased and floured 9" x 13" pan. Bake at 325° F. for 1 hour or until tests done. May be served cold or warm with whipped nonfat milk. Serves 12.

No frosting is needed for this one!

Carol Heinz-Dooley

Strawberry Dip

1 cup vanilla lowfat yogurt
1 teaspoon finely grated lemon peel
1 teaspoon lemon juice

½ cup powdered sugar
Fresh strawberries with stems

Place all ingredients in a bowl, except strawberries, and beat until light and well blended. Chill well. Place in small serving bowls and surround with large fresh strawberries with stems. Serves 6.

This is a very fast and delicious dessert. I serve it in an egg cup on a bread and butter plate.

Milly Powell

Ginger Fruit Compote

1 orange, peeled, sectioned and cut into chunks
1 red delicious apple, cored, cut into chunks
1 banana, peeled and sliced

1 cup seedless grapes
½ cantaloupe, peeled and cut into chunks
2 teaspoons candied ginger, finely chopped
1 cup orange juice

Prepare all fruits and mix gently with candied ginger. Pour orange juice over all fruits. Make sure apple chunks and banana slices are well coated to prevent darkening. Chill until serving time. Serves 4-6.

This is good as a light dessert or as part of a special brunch. Fresh, seasonal fruits can be substituted as desired.

Barbara Gershman

Buttercup Peaches

8 peach halves, well drained (canned, water or juice packed, no syrup)
½ cup rice krispies

½ cup brown sugar substitute
¼ cup margarine

Topping: Cinnamon Sour Cream Sauce

1 cup sour cream or plain lowfat yogurt
2 tablespoons sugar
½ teaspoon cinnamon (or more to suit your taste)

¼ teaspoon nutmeg (or more to suit your taste)

Place drained peaches, cut side up in baking dish. Combine margarine, brown sugar, and rice krispies and sprinkle over peaches. Bake 15 minutes at 425° F. Serve warm with Cinnamon Sour Cream Sauce. Serves 8.

215 calories per serving with topping; 140 calories without.

This is actually my daughter Mary Wenck's recipe (she too is a home economist) and she often made it for the family when she was at home. She still makes it when she comes to visit. It is quick and easy, nutritious and delicious!

Dorothy A. Wenck

88

Ambrosia Cream Puffs

½ cup orange juice
1 cup plain lowfat yogurt
1 egg white
Cream puffs

1 tablespoon cornstarch
1 medium banana, finely chopped
2 tablespoons sugar
2 tablespoons shredded coconut, toasted

In saucepan blend orange juice and cornstarch. Cook and stir until thickened and bubbly. Remove from heat; cool slightly. Fold in yogurt and banana. Chill. Beat egg white with sugar to stiff peaks. Fold into yogurt mixture. Spoon into cream puffs. Garnish with toasted coconut. Put tops on puffs. Serves 8.

132 calories per serving.

Cream Puffs

2 tablespoons butter or margarine
½ cup sifted all-purpose flour
2 eggs

½ cup boiling water
⅛ teaspoon salt

In saucepan melt butter in boiling water. Add flour and salt all at once; stir vigorously. Cook and stir until mixture forms a ball that doesn't separate. Remove from heat; cool slightly. Add eggs, one at a time, beating after each addition until smooth. Drop by heaping tablespoons, 3 inches apart, on lightly greased baking sheet. Bake at 450° F. for 15 minutes. Reduce heat to 325° F.; bake 10 minutes. Remove from oven; cut off tops. Turn oven off; return cream puffs to oven to dry, 20 minutes. Cool on rack. Makes 8.

Carol Heinz-Dooley

Cantaloupe "Ice Cream"

½ medium cantaloupe, peeled and cubed
½ cup evaporated skimmed milk

Artificial sweetener to equal 4 teaspoons sugar
½ teaspoon vanilla or butter pecan extract

Freeze cantaloupe cubes. Combine remaining ingredients in a blender. Blend until smooth. Add frozen cantaloupe. Blend until smooth. Serves 1.

If you like cantaloupe this is so-so-so good!

Roseanne Bye

Pineapple Cheese Cake

½ medium pineapple, cut into chunks
1 cup water
1 cup dietetic creme flavored beverage
2 envelopes unflavored gelatin
⅛ teaspoon salt

1 teaspoon vanilla
1⅓ cups part skim Ricotta cheese or lowfat cottage cheese
Artificial sweetener to equal 3 table-spoons sugar, or to taste

In a saucepan boil the pineapple and water for 20 minutes. Pour beverage into a bowl. Sprinkle gelatin on top. Stir in hot pineapple and cooking liquid. Chill until partially set. Combine partially set mixture in a blender with all remaining ingredients. Blend until smooth. Pour into a cake pan and chill until firm. Divide equally into two portions. Serves 2.

Note: For a topping; toast 2 slices white enriched bread. Make toast into crumbs in a blender. Add cinnamon and artificial sweetener to taste. Blend. Sprinkle crumb mixture evenly over cheese cake before refrigerating.

This is easy to prepare, delicious and low-calorie. You can't lose!

Roseanne Bye

Crustless Pumpkin Pie

3 eggs
¾ cup honey
½ teaspoon ginger
½ teaspoon nutmeg
½ teaspoon cinnamon

½ teaspoon salt
1¾ cups pumpkin
1 cup undiluted skimmed evaporated milk

Beat eggs slightly. Add honey, spices, salt, and pumpkin. Mix well, then add undiluted evaporated milk. Butter or oil a deep 9-inch pie pan. Pour pumpkin custard into pan. Bake at 325° F. (slow) one hour or until knife blade comes out clean. Cool thoroughly before cutting. Serve in pie shaped wedges, topped with honey-sweetened whipped cream, if desired. Serves 8.

Low in calories. A good source of vitamin A.

Mona Schafer Reed

Belgian Waffles with Strawberries

4 egg whites
1 cup unbleached flour
1¼ cups skim milk
1 teaspoon vanilla extract

2 cups sliced fresh strawberries
2 teaspoons undiluted frozen apple juice concentrate

Beat egg whites until stiff peaks form. In another bowl, combine the flour, milk, and vanilla until smooth; then fold the mixture through the beaten egg whites, taking care not to break down the air bubbles. Spoon the batter into a hot nonstick waffle iron and bake. Meanwhile, combine ½ cup each of the sliced strawberries and the apple juice in an electric blender and process the two into a smooth sauce; pour it over the remaining sliced strawberries and serve as a topping with the waffle. Serves 4.

A fast favorite with family and friends. A real reputation maker!

Karin Haydt

Peach Angel Fluff

¼ cup sugar
2 envelopes unflavored gelatin
¼ teaspoon salt
1 cup cold water
6 fresh medium peaches, peeled and
   pitted

Lemon juice
4-5 drops Almond extract
4 egg whites
1 envelope low-calorie dessert topping
   mix
8 ladyfingers

In saucepan combine sugar, unflavored gelatin, salt. Add water. Stir over low heat until gelatin is dissolved. Chill until partially set. Cut one peach in half, reserving one half, dipping in ascorbic acid color keeper or lemon juice, mixed with water. Dice remaining peaches; add 2 tablespoons lemon juice and almond extract. Place gelatin mixture, egg whites, and half the diced peaches in a large bowl. Beat with electric mixer until fluffy, about 10 minutes. Chill until partially set. Prepare topping mix following package directions. Fold remaining diced peaches and whipped topping into partially set gelatin. Line sides of 8-inch springform pan with ladyfingers split lengthwise; pour in filling. Chill until firm. Remove sides of pan. Slice reserved peach half; garnish top with peaches. Serves 16.

Very elegant. Only 74 calories per serving.

Carol Heinz-Dooley

Microwave
Magic

Fresh Asparagus with Cashews

4 cups asparagus, diagonally sliced
4 tablespoons butter or margarine

Salt to taste
¼ cup cashews, coarsely, chopped

Place asparagus and butter into baking dish. Microwave on HIGH for 6-8 minutes or until asparagus is tender-crisp. Stir once. Sprinkle with salt. Stir. Garnish with cashews. Serves 4.

One-half cup croutons may be substituted for cashews; a nice crunchy texture.

Mary Ann Sheets

Savory Zucchini

4 cups zucchini (2 medium), cut into chunks
1 onion, thinly sliced
4 eggs, beaten
1½ cups Cheddar cheese, grated (use lowfat cheese for part of total amount)

1 jar (2 ounce) pimiento
½ teaspoon salt
⅛ teaspoon pepper

Place zucchini and onion in 10" x 6" x 2" buttered dish (or fluted quiche dish). Cover with plastic wrap, turning one edge back slightly to vent. Microwave on HIGH 7 minutes. Drain. In a large bowl beat eggs. Add cheese, pimiento, salt and pepper. Pour mixture over zucchini and onions. Cover with paper towel and microwave at MEDIUM HIGH 8-10 minutes turning and removing paper towel after 4 minutes, until center is set. Serves 6.

A colorful as well as tasty dish—a good Christmas vegetable!

Norma Takesian

Crustless Quiche

3 eggs
1 cup evaporated skim milk
½ teaspoon salt
¼ teaspoon nutmeg
1 tablespoon parsley flakes

2 cups (8 ounces) Swiss cheese, grated
½ cup Parmesan cheese, grated
⅔ cup (4 ounces) cubed Canadian-style bacon or cooked ham

In mixing bowl, beat eggs, evaporated milk, salt and nutmeg until well mixed. Stir in parsley, cheeses and Canadian bacon. Pour into six, 6-ounce custard cups. Cook, uncovered, 4-5 minutes (stir after 1 to 2 minutes to move cooked edges to center) or until knife inserted in center comes out clean. Let stand 2 minutes to finish cooking. If desired, unmold on toasted English muffin halves or tomato slices to serve. Serves 6.

The taste of quiche without the crust! Good recipe for a hearty brunch or light supper, served with rolls and fruit.

Virginia Witmer

94

Mini Chile Rellenos

1 can (2 ounce) whole Jalapeno chiles
Lowfat pasteurized cheese
3 eggs, separated

1½ tablespoons all-purpose flour
1 tablespoon oil

Rinse chiles, being careful to remove all seeds. Stuff with sticks of cheese. Set aside. Beat egg whites in small mixing bowl until stiff peaks form. In small bowl, beat yolks with flour. Fold yolk mixture with egg whites. Preheat micro browner on HIGH for 2 minutes. Spread 1 tablespoon cooking oil on browner. Spoon about ¼ cup batter onto each end of browner. Place 1 stuffed chile, on half of batter. Microwave on HIGH for 30 seconds. Fold in half over chile and continue for 15-20 seconds or until set. Repeat to use all batter. (Reheating of Micro Browner takes 30 seconds). If doing a large quantity, make them up ahead, put on a serving platter, and reheat in microwave oven at serving time. Serves 6.

With these mini-omeletes, you can make them to order as your guests are ready or let them help with their selection of fillings. They make a novel appetizer or first course.

Virginia Witmer

Oriental Fish Fillets

2 tablespoons soy sauce
2 tablespoons frozen orange juice con-
    centrate
1 tablespoon lemon juice
1 tablespoon catsup

⅛ teaspoon instant minced garlic or 1
    clove garlic, minced
1 pound fresh or frozen fish fillets, thawed
    (turbot works beautifully)

In 2-quart baking dish, combine soy sauce, orange and lemon juice, catsup and garlic. Arrange fish in dish, turning over to coat with sauce. Cook in microwave with wax paper or plastic wrap on HIGH for 5 minutes or until fish flakes easily. Let stand, covered 2 minutes to finish cooking. Can serve extra sauce over rice. Serves 4.

Recipe can be doubled and cooked in 2-quart (12" x 7") baking dish for 10 minutes. A tangy dish and oh so easy!

Carol Heinz-Dooley

Stuffed Mushrooms

1 pound large fresh mushrooms
3 green onions, sliced
1 tablespoon diet margarine

¼ cup sour cream (may substitute lowfat
    plain yogurt)
1 package (8 ounce) Neufchatel cream
    cheese

Wash mushrooms; remove stem from each cap by twisting. Arrange caps, stem-side-up, in 3-quart (13" x 9") glass baking dish; set aside. Chop stems fine. Place

stems, onions and diet margarine in medium glass mixing bowl. Microwave for 3 minutes on ROAST, or until onions are tender. Stir in sour cream; add cream cheese. Microwave for 2½ minutes, on ROAST, or until cream cheese is softened; stir well. Divide mixture into four (6 ounces each) custard cups. Stir ingredients from one of the variations, below, into each cup. Fill mushroom caps with one of cream cheese mixtures. Microwave for 5-6 minutes, on ROAST, or until hot.

Mexican mushrooms: Add 1 tablespoon chopped green chiles and ¼ cup shredded Monterey Jack cheese to ¼ of basic recipe. Garnish each mushroom with one strip of pimiento.

Italian mushrooms: Add 3 slices of crisp bacon, crumbled, 5 black olives, chopped, ¼ teaspoon oregano leaves and ¼ teaspoon sweet basil leaves to ¼ of the basic recipe. Garnish each mushroom with dried parsley flakes.

French mushrooms: Add ¼ cup crumbled blue cheese and ⅛ teaspoon tarragon leaves to ¼ of basic recipe. Garnish lightly with tarragon leaves.

Indian mushrooms: Add 2 tablespoons flaked coconut and ¼ teaspoon curry powder to ¼ of basic recipe. Garnish with paprika.

Especially colorful for the holidays. Limit yourself to keep calories lower.

Carol Heinz-Dooley

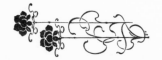

INDEX

97

EGGPLANT CAVIAR, 9
EL POLLO SUPREMO, 65
ENCHILADA OTRA VEZ
  (TURKEY), 62

F

FRENCH HERBED CHICKEN, 64
FRESH ASPARAGUS WITH
  CASHEWS, 94
FROZEN STRAWBERRY
  "DAIQUIRI", 13

G

GAZPACHO DE LOS ANGELES,
  18
GAZPACHO SOUP, 18
GINGER FRUIT COMPOTE, 88
GREEK LEMON SOUP, 17
GREEK MOUSSAKA, 53
GREEN BANANA SOUP, 20
GREEN PEA SALAD, 30
GREEN PEPPER STEAK, 49
GUACAMOLE, 9
"GUACAMOLE", 7

H

HALIBUT RAGOUT, 72
HOLIDAY SALAD BOWL, 24
HONEY BRAN BUD MUFFINS, 35
HONEY FRENCH DRESSING, 27
HOT ASPARAGUS SALAD, 29
HOT SPICED FRUIT SALAD, 29
HOT TOMATO REFRESHER, 12
HOT TURKEY OR CHICKEN
  SALAD, 30

I

ISLAND TERIYAKI, 54

J
JAZZED-UP PORK CHOPS, 59
JELLIED GAZPACHO SALAD, 31

K

KUMQUAT AVOCADO SALAD, 28

L

LEMON PINEAPPLE MOUSSE, 87
LIGHT SEAFOOD SPAGHETTI, 71
LIGHT WEIGHT SOUR CREAM, 26
LIME DRESSING, 25
LO-CAL SALAD DRESSING, 27
LOUISIANA SHRIMP DIP, 8
LOW-CALORIE SOUP, 17
LUMPIA (FROM THE PHILIPPINES),
  6

M

MACARONI ACAPULCO, 58
MAGICAL QUICHE, 42
MARINATED AVOCADO-
  MUSHROOM SALAD, 27
MARINATED CARROT SALAD, 22
MEAT LOAF, 54
MEXICALI SOUFFLE, 44
MINA'S SUGAR FREE CRANBERRY
  RELISH, 81
MINI CHILE RELLENOS, 95
MOO GOO GAI PAN, 64
MORNING GLORY, 12
MUFFIN PAN MEAT LOAVES, 55

N

NOODLE CHEESE CASSEROLE,
  51

W

WATERCRESS SOUP, 16
WHEAT GERM SNACK STICKS, 34
WINNERS SQUASH PIE, 86
WINTER TOMATO SALAD, 23
WONTON SALAD, 27

XYZ

ZESTY ZUCCHINI, 82
ZUCCHINI BREAD, 36
ZUCCHINI CASSEROLE, 79
ZUCCHINI FRITTATA, 76
ZUCCHINI RICOTTA BAKE, 83